The Politics of Federal Grants

THE POLITICS OF FEDERAL GRANTS
by George Hale & Marian Palley

Complimentary Review Copy
Regular Price $7.50

available from publisher only

Congressional Quarterly Inc.
1414 22nd St. N.W.
Washington, D.C. 20037

Politics and Public Policy Series

Advisory Editor

Robert L. Peabody

Johns Hopkins University

The Politics of Federal Grants

George E. Hale

Special Assistant for Intergovernmental Relations
Executive Department, State of Delaware

Marian Lief Palley

Professor of Political Science
University of Delaware

Congressional Quarterly Press

a division of

CONGRESSIONAL QUARTERLY INC.
1414 22nd Street N.W., Washington, D.C. 20037

Jean L. Woy   *Acquisitions Editor*

Lynda McNeil   *Project Editor*

Maceo Mayo   *Production Supervisor*

Richard Pottern   *Cover Design*

Printed in the United States of America

Library of Congress Cataloging in Publication Data

Hale, George E., 1949-
  The politics of federal grants.

  Bibliography: p.
  Includes index.
  1. Grants-in-aid—United States. 2. Intergovernmental fiscal relations—United States. I. Palley,
Marian Lief, 1939- . II. Title.

HJ275.H28   336.1´85   81-960
ISBN 0-87187-161-0   AACR2

Preface

Several years ago we began to study the effects of federal grants on the behavior of grant recipients in state and local government. We saw a system in which the maze of intergovernmental grants for any one policy area was so complex that often the local officials charged with administering a program were not aware of the grants available.

After we completed our initial studies, we began to ask other questions regarding the politics of the intergovernmental grants process. We observed considerable administrative discretion in state agencies regarding such questions as which federal grant options to accept or reject, how to interpret federal program regulations, and how federal funds should be disbursed within states. We did not, however, see a strong part taken by legislators or elected officials. It occurred to us that the system was much like the regulatory process that applies to federal government relations with the private sector. We extended this analogy, and the questions that emerged were, "Who really governs?" and "Does the system work?" It is to these considerations that this volume is addressed.

We also thought it was important to relate the modern grants system to traditional concepts of federalism and to trace the evolution of grants programs through the stages of the policymaking process. In Chapter 1, therefore, we look at federalism and at the history of federal grants in the United States. Our regulatory model is introduced and explained in Chapter 2. Chapters 3 through 5 treat the stages of policymaking—agenda setting, policy adoption, and federal implementation. Chapter 6 discusses the general effects of federal grants on subnational jurisdictions. In Chapters 7 and 8 we examine the politics of federal grants specifically in urban and rural areas. Finally, Chapter 9 summarizes the argument and suggests what implications the grants system may have for policymaking and the federal government.

We hope that this book will be of use both to students of political science and public administration and to practitioners working in intergovernmental relations.

There are several people who were especially helpful to us during the various stages of our research and writing. In particular, we would like to thank Sheldon Edner, David Walker, Deil Wright, Richard Scher, and Albert J. Richter. In addition, we owe thanks to several anonymous reviewers of earlier journal articles. Jeanne Grill, who typed successive drafts of this book as well as the convention papers and journal articles that preceded our work on this volume must be especially thanked for her assistance. Finally, Jean Woy and Lynda McNeil provided us with outstanding editorial assistance. The University of Delaware gave us several grants to help defray the costs of our research efforts.

George E. Hale
Marian Lief Palley

Contents

1

Federalism and Intergovernmental Grants

The nature of the American federal system has changed dramatically during the twentieth century. During the past 15 or 20 years especially, dating roughly from the start of the Great Society era, the pace of change has quickened. As a result, the intergovernmental grants system of the early 1980s bears little resemblance to the grants-in-aid system that existed even as recently as the Kennedy administration. Because of its expanded fiscal and administrative scope, the intergovernmental grants system now stands at the center of national domestic policy. Almost every aspect of domestic service delivery is "intergovernmentalized" today; virtually any state and local program can be aided by one federal grant or another. In some areas the federal government plays an important role as a "banker" government, financing the operations of the state and local agencies without exercising administrative control. Yet in many other areas, public health or environmental quality for example, the provision of basic public services requires extended intergovernmental bargaining, administrative coordination, and interdependent financing.

The significance of the changes in the past two decades is often difficult to assess. Consequently, the intergovernmental grants system bears little resemblance "to the model most Americans carry around in their heads," according to a former deputy mayor of New York City, Edward Hamilton.[1]

To the untrained eye it might appear that America is witnessing the evolution of a centralized system of public financing and policy-making accompanied by a decentralized system of program administration. This analysis is too simple. Politics and administration cannot be so neatly separated. The various roles of government at the national and subnational levels often are characterized not by a division of labor but by overlap and duplication. Representatives of state and local interests—mayors, governors, county officials, and program specialists such as police chiefs and manpower administrators—actively struggle to shape national policy. Conversely, federal administrators often monitor or actually make routine decisions at the state, county, and local levels.

In short, the functions of the three levels of government are no longer distinguishable. Their revenue sources are both interdependent and overlapping, and there often is a wide gulf between the point of decision and the visibility of governmental action. The result is "a vast muddling of the appropriate fiscal, administrative, and servicing roles of governments in the system." [2]

Now more than ever, significant policy changes cannot take place without extensive intergovernmental bargaining and joint funding. This increases the time necessary for coordination and undermines the role of elected officials. Considerable power has shifted to career civil servants who enjoy longer tenure than do most state and local elected officials. Complex networks dominate intergovernmental relations and raise important political and administrative questions. First, it is no longer easy to answer the basic question: "Who governs?" Important policymakers may not be visible or accountable. Second, as more participants become involved in intergovernmental relations, public management becomes increasingly problematic. Thus, any examination of the intergovernmental grants system must ask another question: "Does it work?"

There are many components of the intergovernmentalized American political system. This book is concerned primarily with only one component, federal *grants* to jurisdictions below the national level. More specifically, this book looks at the policy process as it affects the politics of intergovernmental grants and at the impact of those grants on state and local governments.

In Chapter 1 there will be a discussion of the evolution of federalism to provide a better perspective on the contemporary American federal system and the development of the American intergovernmental grants process. We will also look at the economic and political factors which have influenced the evolution of the contemporary grants system.

In Chapter 2 we will introduce a framework for understanding the contemporary grants process. More specifically, we propose that the politics of the intergovernmental grants process closely resembles regulatory politics as it affects private sector operations.

In Chapters 3 through 6 we discuss the numerous questions about the policy process surrounding federal grants and the impact of federal assistance. These chapters assess basic issues of governmental accountability and performance. After following the policy cycle through agenda building, policy adoption, federal implementation, and state and local implementation, the discussion will turn to an examination of federal aid from the point of view of local officials. Additionally, these chapters investigate the role played by the president; Congress; departmental political executives; career civil servants, including officials in regional offices; state and local elected officials and administrators representing school districts, cities, towns, counties, states, and regional organizations; as well as officials of public and functional interest groups. In Chapters 7 and 8 we examine some of the problems relating to intergovernmental grants experienced in metropolitan and nonmetropolitan jurisdictions.

FEDERALISM

The Idea and Evolution of Federalism

Although students of contemporary federalism often accept the American federal system as the model for other federal systems, it is a mistake to conclude that federalism was developed in the eighteenth century by our nation's founders. Furthermore, the concept of contemporary federalism is difficult to define. Any federal system, however, provides a means "of organizing power and the relations that flow from it. . . . Most particularly, it is a means for sharing power in political and social systems." [3] According to Daniel Elazar, "Federalism may be defined as the mode of political organization that unites separate polities within an overarching political system in such a way as to allow each to maintain its own fundamental integrity." Federalism is more than structure; it is a mode of both social and political behavior which involves "a commitment to partnership and cooperation" by both the individuals and the institutions that seek to preserve their own integrity. [4]

There are several kinds of federalism. Martin Diamond suggested that, at the very minimum, there are three ideal types: Greek polis-federalism, small republic federalism, and decentralist-federalism. [5] Greek polis-federalism, the minimal federal union established on the Greek peninsula among ancient city-states, envisioned the autonomous city-state as governing itself. Any larger governing unit was thought to destroy the "good life." Nonetheless, the Greeks recognized that certain functions, such as those relating to war and common defense, could not be performed well by small, autonomous units. To rectify this situation the Greeks established a minimal federal union—they viewed federalism mainly as a prerequisite to a successful foreign policy.

In practice, federal principles can be traced back to the ancient Israelites as well as to the Greeks. In the beginning of the thirteenth century B.C. the Israelites employed national federalism to maintain the unity of their several tribes.[6] During the Middle Ages the antecedents of modern federalism appeared in such diverse societies as Spain—until Aragon and Castille joined together under Ferdinand and Isabella—and the Swiss cantonal confederation of 1291. Many medieval towns joined together for mutual defense and assistance as did the Jewish communities of this era. During the Reformation, federalism developed as a social construct in Switzerland, Scotland, The Netherlands, England, and sections of France and Germany. (However, the term *federal* was not invented until 1645. It is a derivation of the Latin word *foedus,* meaning covenant.)[7] Thus, principles of federalism were rooted in the prenational consciousness of the American colonists. Many colonists seemed to assume that their relationship to Britain was a federal system. The British harbored no such notions, however, and this conflict resulted in the American Revolution and the development of the new nation.[8]

Small republic federalism, described by Montesquieu, evolved from polis-federalism and subsequently influenced the framers of the American federal system. Similar to polis-federalism in many respects, it reflected changed attitudes toward the underlying value of the small country. While the Greeks valued smallness as essential for protecting virtue and the "good life," Montesquieu and others conceived smallness only as a precondition of republicanism, republican liberty, and citizenship. Thus, the reason for preserving the autonomy of small governing units was somewhat reduced, and the arguments against the enlargement of central authority became less persuasive.[9]

A third concept of federalism, decentralist-federalism, emerged in the United States as a result of the interplay of political forces at the Constitutional Convention of 1787 and existing federalist theory. American federalism, according to Diamond, is:

> a national system that is profoundly (and valuably) tilted toward decentralization by its unique admixture of elements of authentic federalism. If there is to be considered a federal system at all, we may then term it decentralist-federalism, a pallid successor to polis-federalism and small-republic federalism.[10]

Alexis de Tocqueville, in his *Democracy in America,* described the American federal union: "(e)vidently this is no longer a federal government, but an incomplete national government, which is neither exactly national nor exactly federal."[11] Similarly, James Madison in *Federalist 39* asserted "(t)he proposed constitution . . . is, in strictness, neither a national nor a federal constitution, but a composition of both."[12]

When Americans developed a federal union in a modern, postfeudal society, they were relatively free from foreign entanglements and isolated from other nations. They were thus insulated from the pressures that encourage completely centralized power. The original formulation of the American federal system, often called dual federalism, rested on an allocation of powers between the national and state governments. While preserving substantial powers for the state governments, the original design presupposed strong national power.

The term federalism is sometimes used to describe the two- or three-tiered pattern of intergovernmental relations, the observed division of power and activity within a system.[13] Actually, federalism is a more complex construct in which there are always three basic features: 1) written constitutions, 2) diffusion of power among substantially self-sustaining centers, and 3) an areal division of power. This generally accepted definition of federalism was stated by K.C. Wheare: "By federal principle I mean the method of dividing powers so that the general and regional governments are each, within a sphere, coordinated and independent."[14] In addition to these basic characteristics common to all federal systems, several supportive elements exist in successful federal experiments. Direct lines of communication between units, geographic necessity (such as the need to maintain a joint defense against common enemies), relative equality in population and wealth among the constituent units (or, at a minimum, balanced geographic or numerical inequality), permanent internal boundaries, constituent representation in the national legislature, and a decentralized political party system are common to all federal systems. The American federal union contains all of these basic and supportive components.

The American Constitution and Federalism

"As a political principle, federalism has to do with the constitutional diffusion of power so that the general government and the various constituent groups of a polity share in the processes of policy-making and administration by right, while the activities of governments are conducted in such a way as to maintain their respective integrities."[15] These considerations were certainly relevant to the framers of the United States Constitution who established two levels of power and authority but did not separate totally the appropriate functions of the general government (federal) and the various constituent groups (states). In order to establish some frame of reference for the functions of the levels of government, the authors of the Constitution provided that specific powers be delegated to the Congress. In Article I Section 8 of the U.S. Constitution, 17 specific grants of power were provided as well as the power:

> To make all Laws that shall be necessary and proper for carrying into Execution the foregoing Powers, and all other Powers vested

by this Constitution in the Government of the United States or in any Department or Officer thereof.

This constitutional provision, known as the *necessary and proper clause,* along with Article VI, the *national supremacy clause,* has provided for federal power in a wide sphere of activity. The national supremacy clause states that:

> This Constitution, and the Laws of the United States which shall be made in Pursuance thereof; and all Treaties made, or which shall be made, under the Authority of the United States, shall be the supreme Law of the Land; and the Judges in every State shall be bound thereby, any Thing in the Constitution or Laws of any State to the Contrary notwithstanding.

To maintain a balance between these constitutional proclamations of federal power, and to preserve the political integrity of the states, the Tenth Amendment to the United States Constitution reserved certain powers for the states. Thus, the Tenth Amendment states that,

> The powers not delegated to the United States by the Constitution, nor prohibited by it to the States, are reserved to the States respectively, or to the people.

The powers delegated or reserved to levels of government were generally vague—though it is significant that very specific limits on the states regarding the national defense, foreign trade, the postal system, and the monetary system were outlined. Some concurrence of powers in overlapping spheres was incorporated into the Constitution. For example, a right of citizenship as central as the right to vote is shared by the levels of government, and the election of national officials depends upon state implementation of constitutional requirements. In this way there is federal dependence on state actions. There is also state dependence on federal actions, such as federal regulation of the banking industry and enforcement of interstate commerce laws.[16]

The Constitution reflected the concerns of its framers that governmental power be decentralized; their specific applications of federal principles provided for such dispersion of power. In the almost 200 years since its ratification, the ideas of decentralization and centralization have coexisted in American political consciousness. The complex system of concurrent powers and intergovernmental grants that has evolved in the United States seems to attest to the compatability of these otherwise seemingly divergent ideas. We will now examine the changing role of intergovernmental grants in the American federal system.

THE EVOLUTION OF INTERGOVERNMENTAL GRANTS

The Early Period (1789-1862)

In the period prior to the Civil War there was only limited national involvement in the activities of the separate states. Although a few programs related to the national defense, foreign policy, currency, and postal services existed, the Tenth Amendment to the Constitution was seen as governing many relationships between the federal government and the states. A literal interpretation of the Tenth Amendment, for example, caused President Franklin Pierce to veto legislation in 1854 providing land to the states for facilities for the mentally handicapped. In his veto message, Pierce asserted:

> I cannot find any authority in the Constitution for making the Federal Government the great almoner of public charity throughout the United States. . . . It would in the end be prejudicial rather than beneficial to the noble offices of charity, to have the charge of them transferred from the States to the Federal Government.[17]

During this period in American history the states rights movement rose to power. In addition, the Supreme Court under Chief Justice Taney increasingly became protective of state power. Nonetheless, several land grants to the states took place during this period. One, the Northwest Ordinance of 1787, even dates from the preconstitutional period. Yet these grants were infrequent and were not tied to specific national conditions or requirements.

From Land Grants to Monetary Grants (1862-1911)

The states rights movement culminated in the southern states' secession from the Union and the outbreak of the Civil War. Although the extreme nullification position failed in 1865 when the South lost the war, states rights continued as a viable position in American politics. It remains alive today; new national initiatives still encounter resistance. The start of a new era in federalism was marked by the congressional passage of the Morrill Act of 1862. This legislation granted portions of public lands to each state. The profits from the land sales supported public institutions of higher education, which became known as the land grant colleges. Congress required these schools to provide training in agriculture and mechanical arts, later adding a requirement for military instruction to respond to the wartime conditions of 1862. The Union Army needed scientists and engineers, and the nation needed farmers to produce food for the Army. Congress also required the states to make annual reports to it on the status of these institutions.[18]

Thus, the Morrill Act established several basic elements of categorical aid: "needed resources were provided in exchange for acceptance of certain minimum standards for a specific purpose." Nevertheless, many of the features of modern grants-in-aid remained absent from this landmark legislation. There were no matching requirements, and states retained control over professional standards, level of support, and curriculum content. No administrative ties with federal agencies existed, and there was no system of federal inspections and audits.[19]

In the closing years of the nineteenth century, Congress began the transition from land grants to monetary grants. In 1879 a program of special aid to the blind was enacted. The Hatch Act in 1887 provided for the first annual cash grants to the states for the creation of agricultural experiment stations. Along with the appearance of these monetary grants came increased administrative supervision. The poor administration of the prior land grant programs led Congress in 1894 to authorize the secretary of Agriculture to audit agricultural experiment station accounts. Additionally, the Morrill Act of 1890 required the secretary of the Interior to certify each state's eligibility for the annual grant and to withhold payments if the conditions of the grant were not met. Although these monetary grants foreshadowed significant changes in American federalism, by 1902 they provided less than 1 percent of all state and local revenue and amounted to only 1 percent of all federal expenditures.[20]

The Development of Categorical Grants (1911-1964)

The third stage in the evolution of the intergovernmental grants process began just prior to World War I and lasted until the mid-1960s when the number of social programs rapidly expanded during the Johnson administration. During this 50-year period there was a steady growth in the number and scale of federal grants. Additionally, new federal controls helped transform the nature of American federalism and the federal grants process. This era in American federalism dates roughly from the ratification of the Sixteenth Amendment to the Constitution in 1913 which provided that

> The Congress shall have power to lay and collect taxes on incomes, from whatever source derived, without apportionment among the several States, and without regard to any census or enumeration.

Because this new elastic source of revenue provided automatic growth in tax collections, tax collections grew at the same rate as did the economy. By 1922 the income tax accounted for 60 percent of national receipts. This set the stage for increased sharing of revenue with the states and localities which were saddled with less elastic taxes.

Once the income tax took effect, Congress had the ability to enact new and broader grants programs than ever before. In 1916 Congress passed the Federal Aid Highway Act, the first major assistance program thoroughly supervised by federal officials. This legislation provided federal aid to the states for road construction based on a funding formula linked to a state's size, population, and rural mail route mileage. States were required to match federal contributions dollar for dollar and also establish a state highway department. By 1917, every state had established the necessary administrative unit; during the 1920s this program accounted for 75 percent of all intergovernmental aid.[21]

Congress enacted several other federal aid programs in the years following passage of the Sixteenth Amendment. The Smith-Hughes Act of 1917 represented the federal government's initial entry into the area of vocational education and thus brought state education under some national scrutiny. The Vocational Rehabilitation Act of 1920 which aided disabled veterans, and the Sheppard-Towner (Maternity) Act of 1921 which provided maternal and infant care, sparked resentment by some state officials who saw these programs as intrusions into areas traditionally reserved for the states.

The Supreme Court subsequently addressed state challenges to the federal grants-in-aid mechanism in its 1923 decisions: *Massachusetts* v. *Mellon* and *Frothingham* v. *Mellon*. The Court held in these cases that " . . . to assume a position of authority over the governmental acts of another and coequal department, (is) an authority which plainly we do not possess." Thus, in two cases where the states sought to enjoin Andrew Mellon, secretary of the Treasury, from spending federal funds to implement the Sheppard-Towner Act, the Supreme Court ruled that it did not have jurisdiction. By failing to consider the merits of the challenge to the constitutionality of the grant-in-aid mechanism, the grant-in-aid program remained intact.[22] The question of the constitutionality of federal grants-in-aid later resurfaced after the passage of the Social Security Act. In 1937 the Supreme Court, in *Steward Machine Co.* v. *Davis*, more decisively upheld such programs than they did in 1923. Justice Cardozo, in the majority opinion, found the Social Security Act to be a cooperative attempt "to find a method by which all these public agencies may work together toward a common end." [23] These decisions encouraged expanded use of the grants-in-aid mechanism as a tool for national policy.

By the time Franklin Roosevelt won the 1932 presidential election, the grants device stood as an established, if controversial, part of American public administration. The number of grants had expanded slowly during the 1920s and the amount of aid available jumped from $12 million in 1913 to $232 million in 1932. More importantly, standard features of later grants became firmly established during those years. For instance, advance approval of state plans, fund distribution based on a formula, matching requirements, and detailed reporting became commonplace grant conditions.[24]

Between 1933 and 1938 the economic conditions of the depression and President Roosevelt's dynamism spurred Congress to enact many new emergency federal grant-in-aid programs. In 1935, the 16 continuing programs established during this period cost $2.2 billion. Many of these emergency programs were terminated in the 1940s, however. Even though some of these programs left no lasting imprint on the intergovernmental landscape, President Roosevelt and the Congress did establish clear precedents for massive use of the federal grants process. Moreover, the most far-reaching program enacted during this period was the Social Security Act of 1935, which remains the cornerstone of the nation's complex social welfare system. In addition to the nationally-based Old Age and Survivors Insurance Program, the Social Security Act established several categorical public assistance programs—Aid to Dependent Children, Aid to the Blind, Old Age Assistance—state unemployment insurance programs, and various programs associated with the Children's Bureau.[25] Each program involved federal provision of funds to the states through various formulas. Federal supervision of grant administration also expanded with the Social Security Act. In order to receive the federal dollars, each state had to comply with more regulations than had previously been the case, most notably, merit system requirements in the recipient state agencies. The planning requirements, the range of program options, and the financial incentive to participate also increased.

Another type of relationship emerged during this period. Not only did the federal government provide increased revenues to the states, but increasingly the depression-weary cities became direct grantees. In 1933, as the cities began to look to the government for assistance, the U.S. Conference of Mayors was formed. This new urban lobby achieved a big victory with passage of the Housing Act of 1937 which established a federal, state, and local partnership in the area of public housing. Local communities could decide whether or not to develop a public housing program—the federal government would support municipal public housing programs if they complied with federal stipulations and if the state enacted the necessary enabling legislation.[26]

During the period from World War II until the Great Society years of expanded social programming, many new federal grant-in-aid programs steadily appeared. Substantial increases in federal aid to states and localities took place, from less than $1 billion in 1940 to $8 billion in 1963. Yet as the Advisory Commission on Inter-governmental Relations notes, "the increases over the period 1942-58 merely kept pace with the growth of the economy, with federal payments to state and local governments holding roughly constant at about 1 percent of the gross national product (GNP)." [27] The most extensive assistance came with the enactment of the Highway Act of 1956, which provided 90 percent federal funding for the interstate highway system. Prior to this time, intergovernmental funding was more likely to be on a 50-50 federal-state matching funds basis, so the 1956 legislation represented a significant change; it was one of the first major reductions in matching requirements.

The increase in the number of categorical grants continued through-out this period, spawning new problems. As early as 1949, when the Hoover Commission on government management issued its report, critics charged that the system was developing in a piecemeal manner. The Hoover Commission found that

> Grant programs are unrelated; they are uncoordinated; and they have developed in a haphazard manner without any one agency—Federal or state—concerned with the overall impact and the overall effects of grants-in-aid upon the general operations of government.[28]

Nonetheless, throughout the Eisenhower administration federal control remained comparatively loose. According to James L. Sundquist of The Brookings Institution, the typical grant helped local governments to attain their own objectives. Additionally, administrative oversight was loose, and many grants were allocated by formula, thereby guaranteeing money to jurisdictions on the basis of demographic or economic factors. Although Sundquist's conclusions do not apply to every program, their validity lies in describing the limits of federal control compared to what came later. The grant conditions, matching requirements, and allocation formulas of the early grants reflected a good deal of federal deference to state and local political leaders.[29]

The Grants Explosion (1964-Present)

During the 1960s and 1970s numerous changes were made in the arrangements available for transferring federal assistance to state and local governments. Categorical grants are the oldest form of federal financial aid and can be used for only specific, narrowly defined activities as illustrated in Table 1-1. These categorical grants can be distributed either by the legislative formula (formula grants) or by competition under agency guidelines (project grants). Although their share of total federal assistance dropped from 98 percent in 1968 to 76 percent in 1977, they clearly remain the most popular form of federal aid.

Table 1-1.   Selected Characteristics of Major Types of Federal Grants.

Type of Grant	Recipient Discretion	Program Scope	Funding Criteria
Categorical			
a. Project	Lowest	Narrow-program	Federal Administrative Review
b. Formula	Low	Narrow-program	Legislative formula
Block	Medium	Broad-functional area	Legislative formula
General Revenue Sharing	High	Broadest-government operations	Legislative formula

The second major type of aid is the block grant, which is distributed by means of a formula. Block grants can be used in broad functional areas, and they allow the recipients more discretion over programming than they have when they receive categorical grants. Block grants became popular in the late 1960s and early 1970s.

The newest type of aid, enacted in 1972, is General Revenue Sharing, which allows money to be distributed by formula to 39,000 general purpose units of government with few restrictions on how the money may be used. According to the Advisory Commission on Intergovernmental Relations (ACIR), in 1978 there were 492 categorical grants, five block grants, and one general revenue sharing program. Changes in the mechanisms for the transfer of funds from the federal to the subnational governments are among the most striking political developments of the last decade. As is shown in Table 1-1, there are important differences in the major characteristics of each type of federal grant.

After Lyndon Johnson was elected president, a major explosion in the number, type, and volume of federal grants and assistance activities took place. In fiscal year 1978 federal aid to states and localities exceeded $80 billion, a tenfold increase from the $8.5 billion in 1963. Federal aid to states and localities represented 7.6 percent of the federal budget in 1960; in fiscal year 1977 it topped 17 percent. Today, as illustrated in Table 1-2, federal aid amounts to more than 25 percent of total state and local expenditures.[30] By 1967 the number of grant-in-aid authorizations rose to 379 from 160 in 1962. This rapid increase in grants between 1962 and 1967 reflected a burst of legislative activity in 1965 and 1966 when 130 new programs appeared. These programs sought to induce state and local governments to move into new fields. Federal administrative supervision increased and matching requirements dropped off to encourage state and local participation. Moreover, during this time, project grants, requiring case-by-case review of applications, became more popular and increased the discretion of federal bureaucrats. From 1964 to 1966, for example, Congress added 160 project grants but only 39 formula grants.[31] In addition to this proliferation of grants and increased national control, the Great Society increasingly bypassed the states by giving grants directly to regional and local governments.

In contrast to the Johnson administration, the Nixon administration tried to arrest the rapid growth in federal aid; grant obligations nevertheless doubled during this period. The major White House intergovernmental initiatives during this time were proposals serving as alternatives to narrow categorical grants. President Nixon's "New Federalism" stressed broader, more flexible grants. Congress responded by enacting general revenue sharing and several new block grants, but these reforms merely slowed down the proliferation of categorical

Table 1-2. Historical Trend of Federal Grants-in-Aid Outlays *(millions of dollars).*

	Composition of Grants-in-Aid			Federal Grants as a Percent of Budget Outlays		
	Total grants-in-aid	*Grants for payments to individuals*	*Other*	*Total*	*Domestic*	*State and local expenditures*
Five-year intervals:						
1950	$ 2,253	$ 1,257	$ 996	5.3	8.8	10.4
1955	3,207	1,623	1,584	4.7	12.1	10.1
1960	7,020	2,479	4,541	7.6	15.9	14.7
1965	10,904	3,931	6,972	9.2	16.5	15.3
1970	24,014	9,023	14,991	12.2	21.1	19.4
Annually:						
1975	49,834	17,441	32,392	15.3	21.3	23.1
1976	59,093	21,023	38,070	16.1	21.7	24.4
1977	68,414	23,860	44,555	17.0	22.7	25.8
1978	77,889	25,981	51,908	17.3	22.9	26.4
1979	82,858	28,765	54,093	16.8	22.4	25.6

SOURCE: Office of Management and Budget, *Special Analysis, Budget of the United States Government, 1981* (Washington, D.C.: U.S. Government Printing Office, 1980), p. 254.

grants, which numbered 442 by 1975. The popularity of project grants did decline during Nixon's White House years, however.

This dominant trend continued during the Carter administration. Funds budgeted for grants jumped dramatically from $58 billion in 1976 to over $82 billion in 1979, and the number of grants reached 492. Table 1-2 shows that approximately 35 percent of 1979 grants went to states and localities to be paid out directly to individuals. Efforts to consolidate grant programs reached a standstill; no new block grants were enacted under either presidents Ford or Carter. Aid to local governments grew as a major part of the system, and regulatory and administrative burdens continued to mount. This proliferation of intergovernmental grants was, in part, a response to economic and political conditions. However, by 1979 there was a slowdown in the rate of increase in dollars expended for federal grants-in-aid. This slowdown was especially severe in its effects on state and local governments. In 1978, almost $77.9 billion was provided by the federal government to subnational jurisdictions; in 1979 the comparable figure was $82.8 billion. When adjusted for inflation, this represented a 5 percent decline in federal aid. In addition, as indicated by the data in Table 1-2, budget outlays for federal grants during 1979 declined as a percentage of both the federal budget and state and local expenditures. Given current economic and political conditions, it seems reasonable to expect that for the foreseeable future there will be no major real increases in federal grants to subnational governments. Certainly President Reagan is unlikely to propose major new grant programs.

ECONOMIC AND POLITICAL CONDITIONS FAVORING THE INCREASES IN GRANTS

Several economic and political variables have influenced the growth of the intergovernmental grants system. The expansion of the welfare state, increased costs of service delivery, and weaknesses in state and local tax bases help explain some of the expansion of the grants system. Politically speaking, the expanding role of special interest groups and program administrators, increased regionalism, and declining influence of political parties have dramatically altered and expanded the grants system.

Economic Conditions

Since the New Deal and the initial expansion of the welfare state, more services have been provided and more services are expected by the American people than ever before. Public education is provided for everyone through grade 12, and, at a substantially subsidized rate, for many citizens through graduate school in the vast state university systems. Vocational and training programs are now provided in public postsecondary vocational and technical school systems in most of the states. Public health costs have increased as have demands that government provide funding to find cures for deadly diseases such as cancer and heart disease. Similarly, costly programs for better roads, better mass transit systems, and cleaner air are demanded from our government.

As more public services are provided, the government's role in society increases. When European immigrants reached American cities in the nineteenth and early twentieth centuries, they received services from political clubs, private charities, settlement houses, and religious organizations. Essential social programs such as low-income housing and unemployment insurance programs did not exist on the federal level. One hundred or even 50 years ago private institutions or individuals provided the necessary services that existed; this is no longer the case.

The very provision of services seems to generate demands for more services. Although these services are costly, most of those Americans who regularly complain about high taxes also seem to want more and better services. Thus, even in the wake of California's 1978 tax revolt and the passage of Proposition 13 and similar tax rebellions in other states, demands for public services remained high. This irony is apparent in the case of health care: 82 percent of those who identified with the Democratic Party in 1978 favored a law or an amendment requiring a balanced federal budget, while at the same time 61 percent favored a government-financed national health insurance program.[32]

Not only have the demands for services increased, so too have the costs. One factor influencing the cost of state and local services has been improvement or expansion of services; another factor is inflation. From 1967 to 1978 there was a 100 percent increase in the Consumer Price Index (CPI). Another condition that has affected the costs of service delivery is the post-World War II baby boom. As the population has increased, the number of potential recipients for services has grown. School systems have expanded to accommodate the needs of growing numbers of children, there are now more old people who are eligible for Medicare, and the numbers of people drawing social security benefits continues to grow. According to a study by The Brookings Institution, the increased size of state and local budgets from 1955 to 1974 was due to all three of these forces: 52 percent due to inflation; 35 percent due to service improvements; and 13 percent due to service expansion or workload changes.[33]

The states and localities have found it increasingly difficult to raise the funds to pay for these services. This is because some very costly programs—such as education—fall directly on state and local jurisdictions. Cities, and to a lesser extent states, have more limited and less elastic tax bases than the federal government. It is increasingly difficult for them to raise the funds necessary to provide essential services. Local jurisdictions raise most of their locally originated revenues by property taxes, special charges, and sales taxes. Although the states use more elastic income taxes, they are politically limited since they compete with each other and with the federal income tax. They also rely heavily on the state sales tax, which barely keeps pace with inflation. One result of this mismatch between the demand for service delivery and the available funds is that states and localities increasingly turn to federal grants-in-aid, and increased bonded indebtedness, as alternatives to politically unpopular budget cuts or tax increases. The dependence on external revenue sources is illustrated by the fact that state and local bonded indebtedness increased from $16 billion in 1945 to $174.5 billion in 1972,[34] and as noted previously, federal intergovernmental aid to states and localities increased from $8 billion in fiscal year 1960 to more than $82 billion in fiscal year 1979.

Political Conditions

In addition to the economic factors, several political developments have contributed to the recent growth and proliferation of federal grants. The strength of the political parties has declined, which has produced a rise in local pressure on national politics. Public Interest Groups (PIGs) have expanded into an intergovernmental lobby, made up of coalitions of state and local administrators and elected officials who support passage of new grants programs.[35] These PIGs should not be confused with public interest groups such as Consumer's Union, the Sierra Club, or Common Cause, which Andrew McFarland characterizes as initiators and maintainers of "the civic-balance of beliefs." McFarland also maintains that

> The political system is seen as complex, fragmented into numerous areas of policy; such policy areas are often controlled by unrepresentative elites, however, who act to further their own special interests to the detriment of the interests of the great majority of the public; such public interests frequently go unrepresented in policy making. . . .[36]

The groups that act to fill this void in the policy process are often identified as public interest groups. Though the PIGs we are discussing may be representing a public good, they are more specifically lobbying organizations for state and local governments and officials.

Since the 1950s there has been a steady trend toward the decline of partisan politics. Today's voters are more knowledgeable and issue-oriented than voters in the Eisenhower era. Ticket splitting has increased during this period, and increasingly larger numbers of voters, more interested and better educated, now are registering as independents, refusing to identify with a major political party. The old Roosevelt coalition has decayed; to many, the old divisions seem irrelevant to the issues of the late 1970s and early 1980s.[37]

The decay of party politics among the voters translates into the decline of partisanship in Congress. Party voting, where a majority of one party opposes a majority of the other, has dropped steadily since the 1950s. Elected congressional leaders hold less influence over the rank-and-file legislators than before. Traditional divisions between the parties are less important to the current electorate and elected officials, and thus an important force in legislative politics has moved to the background.

If politicians don't look to the parties for guidance, to whom are they responsive? When partisanship and national leadership are weak, legislators appear to be more responsive to local pressures. Increasingly, local interests drive the legislative process. When party labels do little to guarantee reelection, constituent service becomes the key to successful incumbency. Often this means bringing federal grants into the district. David Stockman, former Republican Representative from Michigan, openly characterized the grants process as a "social pork barrel." The impact of party is slim because, according to Stockman, "the cost and maintenance of the social welfare spending pipeline that extends to each of the 435 Congressional districts in the nation have now become a central preoccupation of members and their staffs."[38]

The rise of localism and regionalism helps fill the void created by political party decline. Partisan or ideological differences over the appropriate federal role appear when new grants authorizations are debated, but both Republicans and Democrats are interested in increasing federal aid to their districts. The result is a proliferation of grants. When a grant is debated originally, controversy surfaces. The debate over renewal, however, is different. The primary issues in grant renewal become the size of the allocation and distribution of funds among regions and states. Few legislators actually challenge reauthorization and, as David Walker notes, the final votes "usually exceed the two-thirds mark with little evidence of ideology or mere issue orientation reflected in its passage."[39] This, too, helps explain the growth of the intergovernmental grants system.

In addition to the decline of parties and the concomitant rise of localism, a second development has fueled the proliferation and growing complexity of the grants-in-aid device. In the last 40 years a new intergovernmental lobby has appeared.[40] This public sector lobby has filled the void created by the erosion of party discipline. As grants have expanded, subnational officials—governors, mayors, educators, legislators, planners and other program specialists—have gained a greater interest in federal action. Federal officials also have become dependent on local, regional, and state officials for political support. The intergovernmental lobby, with seven main public interest groups—the Council of State Governments, the National Governors' Association, the National Conference of State Legislators, the National Association of Counties, the National League of Cities, the U.S. Conference of Mayors, and the International City Management Association—have responded to what Washington had to offer. This, in turn, has created a new demand for federal grants-in-aid.

PURPOSES OF FEDERAL GRANTS

Before considering the detailed workings of the federal grants system, it is important to examine the goals of intergovernmental programs. Any number of textbook explanations are offered to justify the patterns of grants-in-aid to state and local governments. In practice, however, no single theory or ideology has dominated the development of the intergovernmental grants system. Furthermore, each program has its own constituency, its own formula for allocating funds, and its own administrative requirements. Because the intergovernmental grants system is a patchwork of competing principles and contradictory pressures, it is important to look at the politics of federal grants. Rather than flowing from a single theory, each grant-in-aid, according to Phillip Monypenny of the University of Illinois, "is the product of a specific coalition and the terms of that coalition are evident in the statute and in the administrative practices which result from it."[41] Before examining the twin processes of coalition building and implementation, these textbook justifications, which provide only partial explanations for the patterns of federal assistance to state and local governments, deserve some attention.

One common belief is that federal grants provide for an equalization in the level of public services among the states and localities. This implies that poorer jurisdictions receive larger grants than richer jurisdictions. Critics of this view argue that though legislators may appropriate funds to help solve problems in states or regions other than their own, representatives of rich states are not consistently altruistic. The Advisory Commission on Intergovernmental Relations has noted that "federal aid has not consistently favored the states least able to finance their own public services—the reverse has some times been true—and only a small number of grants (24) explicitly recognize differences in fiscal capacity."[42] Many programs require the recipient jurisdictions to match federal funds with their own resources. Matching requirements often cancel out the impact of any equalization factor. State and local governments with high per capita personal incomes often have high public expenditures and thus can qualify for larger grants through the matching process.

There are several reasons given to explain why federal grants often fall short of the goal of equalizing public services. The first one is that the process of building political support for a program requires that benefits be widely distributed. The more congressional districts that benefit from a program, the greater the probability of finding a supportive legislative majority. This makes it very hard to target or concentrate funds on poor jurisdictions or trouble spots. Second, even when an individual program promotes an equalization of services, sometimes the total allocation of federal aid supports local governments with little concern for differences in fiscal capacity.

Another justification for federal aid is that it provides for a level of services which the national interest requires. Critics of this explanation claim that defenders of almost any intergovernmental program can argue that a national interest is at stake. These critics feel that it is by no means obvious which programs involve national interest or which intergovernmental grants actually promote national interests. Today, every area of domestic policy has been intergovern-mentalized. At one time, according to Elliot Richardson, former secretary of the Department of Health, Education and Welfare,

> narrowly drawn categorical grants legislation would actually advance the targeted national interest. . . .as the number grows, however, a point is reached at which the leverage exerted by a given program has almost completely dissipated: state and local administrators, having a bunch of carrots held out to them, are free to select only those which feed the activities they would have undertaken without any special inducement.[43]

A third justification for federal grants relates to the relative ease with which the national government collects taxes. The national treasury is an efficient tax collector. A variation of this position holds that the federal tax structure's greater progressivity argues for national funding of essential services. This argument, its critics suggest, ignores the fact that most revenue problems faced by subnational governments are largely self-imposed. They claim that property and sales taxes need not be either as regressive or as inelastic as they often are, and that state action often is all that is needed to allow declining cities to tax resources in their suburbs.

Another claim for federal grants is that the involvement of national administrators raises the overall level of performance and competence. Critics of this notion argue that this expectation ignores the fact that the competence of civil servants in many states such as California, New York, Minnesota, and Wisconsin may equal or surpass the expertise of the typical federal agency.[44] They claim that this assumption ignores the growth of the "professional state" that has closed the training and education gap between national and subnational bureaucrats. It is also argued that this justification for federal grants conveniently overlooks the fact that another layer of administration can slow action, increase red tape, encourage buck-passing, and eliminate accountability. Elliot Richardson has argued that "the value of categorical grants has been diminished by ballooning overhead, prolonged delays and endless aggravation." [45]

It is our belief that none of the textbook justifications—equalization, national interest, tax responsiveness, or administrative competence—fully explains the development of intergovernmental grants. Logical consistency and theoretical rigor play but a small role in shaping the sprawling, sometimes contradictory collection of grants to state and local governments. The reason we have so many different grants for such a variety of purposes rests with the nature of political coalitions and with the fragmentation of power in the American federal system. Phillip Monypenny has suggested that

> federal aid programs are an outcome of a loose coalition which resorts to a federal state program, because it is not strong enough in individual states to secure its program, and because it is not united enough to be able to achieve a wholly federal program against the opposition which a specific program would engender.[46]

Grant programs, then, must be viewed as the product of political compromises. Each is the product of a unique political coalition reacting to contemporary developments and public opinion. Only points of agreement are written into law; points of disagreement must be resolved during the implementation of public policy. Uniformity is lacking in the implementation of federal grant programs because federal grants do not represent the triumph of one political theory. Rather, each grant program reflects a balancing of support and opposition. If one level of government assumed all responsibility for a program, these programs might be more consistent or straightforward, but it is unlikely that governmental functions would be so neatly sorted out. Individuals and groups press for a federal role if the states prove to be unresponsive to their pleas, and state and local governments continue to play important roles if no consensus on the role of the federal government appears. To understand the development of the contemporary grants system, it is necessary to turn away from textbook justifications and look at the policymaking process and the compromises between the competing justifications for federal assistance to state and local governments.

NOTES

1. Edward K. Hamilton, "On Nonconstitutional Management of a Constitutional Problem," *Daedalus,* 107 (Winter 1978): 122.
2. David B. Walker, "A New Intergovernmental System in 1977," *Publius,* 8 (Winter 1978): 133.
3. This section relies heavily on Daniel J. Elazar, "Federalism," reprinted from *Encyclopaedia Britannica* (Jerusalem: Jerusalem Institute for Federal Studies, 1978), pp. 1-6.
4. Ibid., p. 2.
5. Martin Diamond, "The Ends of Federalism," *Publius,* 3 (Fall 1973): 129-152.
6. Elazar notes that the record of these efforts is presented in the Bible in the books of Joshua, Judges, Samuel, and Ezekiel. See Elazar, "Federalism," p. 2.
7. Daniel J. Elazar, "Civil War and the Preservation of American Federalism," *Publius,* 1 (1971): 57.
8. Elazar, "Federalism," p. 3.
9. Diamond, "The Ends of Federalism," p. 133.
10. Ibid., pp. 135-136.
11. Ibid., p. 151.
12. Ibid., p. 133.
13. Samuel H. Beer, "The Modernization of American Federalism," *Publius,* 3 (Fall 1973): 50. Beer suggests that there are two other meanings of federalism. He notes that federalism refers to "the jurisdic device of giving exceptional legal protection to the powers of governments of territorial subdivision of a polity"; also "federalism refers to certain attitudes deeply embedded in the political culture of a country."
14. Kenneth C. Wheare, *Federal Government,* 4th ed. (New York: Oxford University Press, 1964), p. 10.
15. Daniel J. Elazar, "First Principles," *Publius,* 3 (Fall 1973): 3; also see Elazar, *American Federalism: A View From the States* (New York: T. Y. Crowell, 1966), Chapter 2.
16. Daniel J. Elazar, "Federalism and Intergovernmental Relations," in *Cooperation and Conflict—Readings in American Federalism,* ed. D. Elazar, R. B. Carroll, E. L. Levine, and D. St. Angelo (Itasca, Ill.: F. E. Peacock Publishers, 1969), p. 12.
17. Ralph E. Pumphrey and Muriel W. Pumphrey, *The Heritage of Social Work* (New York: Columbia University Press, 1961), p. 133.
18. Advisory Commission on Intergovernmental Relations (ACIR), *Categorical Grants: Their Role and Design (A-52)* (Washington, D.C.: U.S. Government Printing Office, 1977), p. 15.
19. Ibid.
20. Ibid., p. 16.
21. Ibid.
22. Harold W. Chase and Craig R. Ducat, *Constitutional Interpretation* (St. Paul, Minn.: West Publishing Co., 1974) pp. 72-73.

23. Steward Machine Co. v. Davis, 201 U.S. 548 (1937).
24. ACIR, *Categorical Grants,* pp. 16-17.
25. Arthur J. Altmeyer, *The Formative Years of Social Security* (Madison, Wis.: University of Wisconsin Press, 1966), Chapter 1.
26. Marian Lief Palley and Howard A. Palley, *Urban America and Public Policies* (Lexington, Mass.: D. C. Heath & Co., 1977), p. 165.
27. ACIR, *Categorical Grants,* p. 23.
28. The Commission on the Executive Branch of Government, *Federal-State Relations, A Report to Congress* (Washington, D.C.: U.S. Government Printing Office, 1949), p. 30.
29. James L. Sundquist with David W. Davis, *Making Federalism Work* (Washington, D.C.: Brookings Institution, 1969), pp. 3-5.
30. Advisory Commission on Intergovernmental Relations, *The Intergovernmental Grant System: An Assessment and Proposed Policies* (Washington, D.C.: Advisory Commission on Intergovernmental Relations, 1978), p. 3.
31. ACIR, *Categorical Grants,* p. 25.
32. "Policy Views of Voters and Candidates," *The New York Times/CBS News Poll, New York Times,* November 11, 1978, p. A21.
33. Emil M. Sunley, Jr., "State and Local Governments," in *Setting National Priorities: The Next Ten Years,* ed. Henry Owen and Charles L. Schultze (Washington, D.C.: Brookings Institution, 1976), p. 379.
34. U.S., Department of Commerce, Bureau of the Census, *Government Finances in 1971-1972,* Series GF-72, No. 5 (Washington, D.C.: U.S. Government Printing Office, 1973), p. 19.
35. Samuel H. Beer, "The Adoption of General Revenue Sharing," *Public Policy* 24 (1976): 127-195.
36. Andrew S. McFarland, *Public Interest Lobbies* (Washington, D.C.: American Enterprise Institute, 1976), pp. 8-9.
37. Everett C. Ladd, Jr. and Charles Hadley, *Transformations of the American Party System: Political Coalitions from the New Deal to the 1970s* (New York: W. W. Norton & Co., 1975).
38. David A. Stockman, "The Social Pork Barrel," *The Public Interest,* 39 (Spring 1975): 12.
39. David B. Walker, "The Balanced Budget Movement: A Political Perspective," *Intergovernmental Perspective* 5 (Spring 1979): 19.
40. Donald Haider, *When Governments Come to Washington* (New York: Free Press, 1974).
41. Phillip Monypenny, "Federal Grants-In-Aid to State Governments: A Political Analysis," *National Tax Journal,* 13 (March 1960): 15.
42. David B. Walker, "Federal Aid Administrators and the Federal System," *Intergovernmental Perspective* 3 (Fall 1977): 11.
43. Elliot Richardson, *The Creative Balance* (New York: Holt, Rinehart, & Winston, 1976), p. 204.
44. Daniel J. Elazar, "The New Federalism: Can The States Be Trusted?" *The Public Interest* 35 (Spring 1974): 89-102.
45. Richardson, *The Creative Balance,* p. 204.
46. Monypenny, "Federal Grants-In-Aid," p. 15.

2

A Regulatory Model
of the Grants Process

We believe that the politics of the intergovernmental grants system today resembles the regulatory relationship that we see between the federal government and the private sector. In this chapter, we will look briefly at the use of models in the social sciences and then at the justification for employing a regulatory model to help understand the political processes surrounding the federal intergovernmental grants process.

MODELS IN THE SOCIAL SCIENCES

"A model is a simplified picture of the real world. It has some of the characteristics of the real world, but not all of them. It is a set of interrelated guesses about the world. Like all pictures, a model is simpler than the phenomena it is supposed to represent or explain." [1] We use the word *model* as a generic term for a "systematic set of conjectures about real world observations." [2] Thus a model may express a simple and approximate verbal statement (e.g., deficit spending causes inflation), a set of mathematical equations, or an elaborate computer program. It is possible for a model to be expressed as a physical structure. In any case, models are approximate representations, and thus simplifications of relationships that are assumed to exist between policies and their consequences. [3] Models vary both in their rigor and in the confidence we can place in them.

In the social sciences there are some basic assumptions that underlie the use of all models. Thomas Dye has suggested that all models should

1) simplify and clarify our thinking about government and politics,
2) identify important political forces in society,
3) communicate relevant knowledge about political life,
4) direct inquiry into politics, and
5) suggest explanations for political events and outcomes. [4]

Models are useful analytic tools though "the theory must specify more or less exactly the nature of the ideal conditions so that the investigator can determine whether or not these are being approximated to a reasonable degree."[5] In the remainder of this chapter an interrelated set of assumptions about the nature of the intergovernmental grants process will be presented and hypotheses regarding its similarities to the political process affecting regulation of private sector activities will be provided. In the remainder of the book the policy process surrounding the development and implementation of federal grants to state and local governments will be traced, which will provide evidence for judging the adequacy of this regulatory model.

TRADITIONAL MODELS OF INTERGOVERNMENTAL RELATIONS

Before proceeding with an analysis of intergovernmental policy-making, it is important to examine several models for viewing federal-state-local relations. As suggested previously, models are important because they identify central questions. They also provide a framework for analyzing data, and for integrating a number of apparently unrelated developments. Since we are focusing on a complex process that still remains a murky area within both political science and public administration, a framework helps develop concepts and identify trends.

We suggest that the contemporary intergovernmental grants process can be compared with regulatory politics. We do not intend to use this model in a heavy-handed manner. It is introduced here and evaluated at the end of the book in order to help the reader examine a complex process; we think it helps link together developments at the various stages of the policy process.

It is important to look at the various ways other political scientists have viewed intergovernmental relations. Here let us note that our goal is already ambitious—to explain the politics of the federal grants system. Accordingly, we will not try to accomplish more than this; many topics and varieties of intergovernmental relations—interstate, state-local, and interlocal—will not be examined. If all of these important issues were covered in such a short book, the salient issues and changing dynamics involving federal aid might be obscured.[6]

Layer Cake Model

Over the years, various models of intergovernmental relations attempted to answer the questions "Who governs?" and "Does it work?" As the nature of the American federal system changed dramatically during the twentieth century, so too did the models used by political scientists. It can be argued that the models proposed are incomplete, in that they address only components of the intergovernmental system. However, since they have been used as key organizing concepts, it is important to understand them.

Traditionally, the American federal system was viewed as a *layer cake,* with each layer separate and discrete from the other levels of government.[7] Thus, the national government was the top layer, and the states with their local governments (politically though not constitutionally) were the second and third layers.

This view recognized that the Constitution provided for a separation between the federal and state governments. As explained in Chapter 1, for well over a century the functions of the various levels of government were largely, though not totally, distinguishable and separate.

Marble Cake Model

During the Depression era, national recovery programs increasingly involved the states as administrators of federal policies. This burst of activity accelerated the slow development of intergovernmental programs that was already taking place. Similarly, local governments increasingly turned to the states for assistance. American federalism underwent a transformation from a layer cake to a system of shared responsibilities and joint action. During the 1950s, Morton Grodzins coined the metaphor *marble cake federalism,* which captured the inadequacy of the older notion of the separation of national, state, and local powers. Grodzins argued that:

> The American form of government is often, but erroneously, symbolized as a layer cake. A far more accurate image is the rainbow or marble cake, characterized by an inseparable mingling of differently colored ingredients, the colors appearing in vertical and diagonal strands and unexpected whirls. As colors are mixed in the marble cake, so functions are mixed in the American federal system.[8]

Indeed, by the middle of the twentieth century it was difficult to find any governmental activity that failed to involve all three levels of government. Federal grants were only the most obvious examples of areas where functions were shared. Grodzins argued that, "even in the absence of joint financing, federal-state-local collaboration is the characteristic mode of action." [9]

Picket Fence Model

Although the marble cake analogy captured the new complexity of American federalism, the emphasis on cooperation and shared responsibilities obscured other features of the intergovernmental grants system that were evolving. In the late 1960s another metaphor, *picket fence federalism,* was coined by Terry Sanford, former governor of North Carolina, to emphasize the political implications of the new intergovernmental grants system. According to Sanford:

> the lines of authority, concerns and interests, the flow of money and the direction of programs runs straight down like a number of pickets stuck into the ground. There is, as in a picket fence, a connecting cross slat, but that does little to support anything. In this metaphor it stands for the governments. It holds the pickets in line; it does nothing to bring them together.[10]

The picket fence model makes two basic and interrelated assertions. First, control and initiative runs from federal administrators to their state and local counterparts. Second, extensive bureaucratic linkages and alliances cross levels of government, primarily through grant-in-aid programs, and reduce the role of elected officials.

At the present time, the picket fence model is a key organizing concept for the study of intergovernmental relations. However, given the increasing complexities of the intergovernmental policy process that developed with the introduction of new grant mechanisms and greatly expanded federal funding in the 1970s, it now appears to be only a partial interpretation of the forces at work. The picket fence assumptions overstate the role of federal officials by ignoring the two-way nature of bargaining and compromise between national and subnational officials. Second, these assumptions underestimate both federal administrative fragmentation and the political clout of state and local officials. Furthermore, like other models, the picket fence analogy concentrates on the issue of "Who governs?" largely at the expense of the day-to-day operations of the grants system.

THE REGULATORY MODEL

Both the marble cake and picket fence explanations make important points about earlier periods in the evolution of the intergovernmental policy process. Also, the models emphasize that functions are not neatly sorted out among levels of government and that administrators play a central role in the conduct of intergovernmental relations. However, it seems that a better way to describe the intergovernmental grants system is to compare it to the regulatory politics that operate in relation to the private sector.

The value of suggesting a regulatory model as a description of intergovernmental politics is that it stresses fundamental political relationships. It helps to link intergovernmental relations with broader patterns of interest group and regulatory politics that will be familiar to many readers. We are not suggesting that there is only one pattern of regulatory politics that exists for the private sector. Similarly, we are not proposing that only one pattern of behavioral interactions influences the intergovernmental grants policy process. Rather, in both arenas the process is extremely complex and subject to constant change. By introducing this analogy, we hope to link the stages of the policy process in a way that prevents the descriptive material from driving out concepts.

In order for a model of regulatory policies to clarify the operations of federal aid it is important to identify the central features of government regulation of business. Three characteristics stand out: 1) private interest groups play an important role; 2) governmental controls may be indirect as well as direct; and 3) both the regulatory agency and the regulated industry become interdependent. Similar dynamics seem to prevail in the intergovernmental grants arena.

Most models of regulatory politics acknowledge that groups outside government often make demands for government activity. Typically, students who study the effects of interest groups focus on corporations, trade associations, and labor unions. Yet state and local governments and officials also act as interest groups seeking both financial support and regulatory concessions from higher levels of government. As the scope of financial assistance expanded during the 1960s and 1970s, more and more people were drawn into Washington's magnetic field by the promise of money or the threat of regulation. During the 1960s, for example, large cities mobilized their forces in Washington; in the early 1970s there was a dramatic expansion of legislative activity by the National Association of Counties. More recently, neighborhood associations and small cities have formed lobbying organizations to protect their interests in both the halls of Congress and the corridors of the bureaucracy.[11]

The modes of operation of public and private sector organizations have increasingly converged to the point where they resemble one another in important ways. According to Samuel Beer, former president of the American Political Science Association: "in their influence on public policy, certain producers of public goods, namely, subnational governments, moved into positions of influence rather like those occupied by producers of private goods." [12] The comparison to government/business relationships in the regulatory arena helps direct our attention to the important role state and local governments play during the process of setting the agenda for governmental action and influencing legislative behavior.

The politics of business regulatory agencies has long been thought to be dominated by what political scientists call *iron triangles.* These iron triangles are actually coalitions that include the regulated industry, the regulatory agency, and the congressional subcommittee or committees with jurisdiction over the regulated activity. In theory, this trio will arrange things so that policy works to their advantage. They do this largely because the public is diffuse and not well-represented before specialized decisionmaking bodies.[13] Intergovernmental policy-making operates in a very similar fashion; administrative agencies, congressional subcommittees, and specialized state and local groups dominate the multiple arenas of decisionmaking.

Intergovernmental programs and regulatory policies depart from the relatively simple administrative initiatives of more traditional national programs that are administered directly by the federal government. Both involve indirect influence rather than hierarchical or managerial solutions to organizational problems. They represent "command and control" responses, and both aim at affecting the actions of thousands of business firms or units of local government. Each focuses on broad objectives. The formal goals of government regulations are to reduce market domination, alter behavior to curb abuses of public welfare, and establish a national economy. Similarly, grants-in-aid programs are ostensibly designed to reduce fiscal disparities among subnational governments, alter the policies of state and local governments, and establish national programs. Each method of intervention also addresses the "free rider" problem in which voluntary arrangements have allowed some individual firms or governments to avoid paying for their share of collective benefits. In short, both regulatory programs and many intergovernmental grants are far more complex and ambitious than the more traditional government programs. Each represents a fundamental change in the way that government operates.

The regulatory model helps focus our attention on the complex goals and indirect methods associated with many federal grant programs that try to change the behavior of others. In each agency there are limits to federal control; no single agency can monitor all the private transactions by individual businesses just as no grantor agency can fully audit all the expenditures of hundreds or thousands of units of state and local government.

Federal control in each arena is imperfect. Given the clout of private interest groups, and given the complexity of many regulatory actions, most observers agree that, regardless of their original purpose, most regulatory agencies become the protectors or promoters of the regulated interest. According to Pendleton Herring, "the greater the degree of detailed and technical control the government seeks to exert over industrial and commercial interests, the greater must be their degree of consent and active participation."[14] Often the agency is captured outright by those it regulates. In other cases, the process is more subtle. Because programs are so specialized, there are very few places to seek political support. So, the controller may increasingly need the support of the controlled. Similarly, federal agencies often turn to state and local officials for political support. The price for this support often is cooptation and greater delegation of day-to-day administration. Because state and local governments have influence with Congress, administrators will often consult local and state politicians before taking controversial actions. As federal grants increase, so too does the federal government's dependence on the political support and administrative capacity of local and state officials. In the case of both regulatory and grant programs the federal government influences, but also is influenced by those it regulates.

Regulatory administration is also highly political because Congress frequently passes legislation that confers broad discretion upon administrative officials. A good deal of intergovernmental legislation contains broad grants of administrative power. Because these agencies, both regulatory and intergovernmental, have legislative and administrative authority they seem to be especially open to pressures from special interests.

The value of the regulatory analogy is that it places *negotiation, bargaining* and *compromise* at the core of the policy process. This conception is central to many classic studies of intergovernmental relations. According to Grodzins, "a judgment of the relative strengths of the two planes must take heavily into account the influence of one on the other's actions." [15] In short, national and subnational governments are interdependent.

The regulatory analogy, then, serves several important purposes. It helps us focus on the growing role of intergovernmental lobbyists. It points out the complexity of goals and the indirect nature of administrative tools for altering the behavior of thousands of governments. Regulatory politics also provides a framework for interpreting the day-to-day process of compromise as broad legislative mandates are translated into concrete programs in the 50 states and thousands of local governments.

CONCLUSIONS

Despite the growing fiscal importance of federal grants and the increasingly complex problems associated with grants administration, intergovernmental relations remains a murky field within political science and public administration. Existing models point to the joint nature of most government activities and one major consequence of increased federal aid is thought to be the forging of alliances between professional administrators at various levels of government. Grants also reduce the control of elected officials over public agencies. Yet complex allocational and administrative issues remain unexplored. For example, the power of federal officials implied in the picket fence model does not seem to be as strong as many assume. State and local officials are also influential in affecting agenda setting, policy adoption, and implementation.

Most textbook discussions of federal grants ignore the political dynamics and compromises behind each program. We suggest that a better description of the federal aid system is that of regulatory politics similar to the one that operates for the private sector. This model focuses attention on the increased role of state and local lobbyists. It also identifies the problems of indirect program administration as it relates to attempts to alter the behavior of thousands of units of government. Finally, the regulatory analogy focuses on the possibility of cooptation, as well as the interdependence of national and subnational officials.

Developments in the late 1970s resulted in widespread concern about the issues of governmental accountability and performance. Perhaps the complexity of the maze makes it difficult for anyone to exercise control. These problems show no signs of abating. Hence, it is important both to describe the political developments and to offer interpretations that link together numerous, apparently unrelated, developments.

NOTES

1. Charles A. Lave and James G. March, *An Introduction to Models in the Social Sciences* (New York: Harper & Row, Publishers, 1975), p. 3.
2. Ibid., p. 4.
3. Duncan MacRae Jr. and James A. Wilde, *Policy Analysis for Public Decisions* (North Scituate, Mass.: Duxbury Press, 1979), p. 99.
4. Thomas Dye, *Understanding Public Policy,* 3d ed. (Englewood Cliffs, N.J.: Prentice-Hall, 1978), p. 19.
5. Hubert M. Blalock and Ann B. Blalock, *Methodology in Social Research* (New York: McGraw-Hill, 1968), p. 157.
6. There are other books that cover the broad scope of intergovernmental relations. See, for example, Deil Wright, *Understanding Intergovernmental Relations* (North Scituate, Mass.: Duxbury Press, 1978); and Parris Glendening and Mavis Mann Reeves, *Pragmatic Federalism* (Pacific Palisades, Calif.: Palisades Publishers, 1977).
7. Morton Grodzins, "The Federal System," in *American Government: Readings and Cases,* ed. Peter Woll (Boston: Little, Brown & Co., 1972), p. 125.

8. Ibid., p. 125.
9. Ibid., p. 126.
10. Terry Sanford, *Storm Over the States* (New York: McGraw-Hill, 1967), p. 80.
11. See, for example, Rochelle L. Stanfield, "Small Cities Are on the Prowl for Help from Washington," *National Journal* 10 (November 7, 1978): 1597-1601.
12. Samuel Beer, "The Adoption of General Revenue Sharing," *Public Policy* 24 (1976): 165.
13. For a critical review of these theories, see Paul H. Weaver, "Regulation, Social Policy, and Class Conflict," *The Public Interest* 50 (Winter 1978): 45-62.
14. E. P. Herring, *Public Administration and the Public Interest* (New York: McGraw-Hill, 1936), p. 192.
15. Grodzins, "The Federal System," p. 139.

3

Agenda Setting

Before any problem can be solved or any policy formulated, it must come to the attention of the policymakers. It must be defined and possible solutions put forward. The process through which this happens is not well understood, but it is clear that numerous policy actors are involved, including the president, interest groups, members of Congress, the press, and the public. The fragmentation of this process and the differential access of policy actors to agenda setting contributes to a diffuse and complex grants system. We now will focus on some of the participants concerned with intergovernmental grants policy.

This chapter examines the politics of bringing intergovernmental problems to the attention of government decisionmakers and asks two essential questions. Which actors, national or subnational, elected or appointed, public or private, bring intergovernmental problems to the attention of the government decisionmakers? Also, which agenda-setting strategies and external factors help grants proposals receive active and serious attention?

The policy process starts with problem definition, which is followed by the agenda-setting stage. Problem definition is critically dependent on the role of functional specialists and representatives of subnational governments. The strategies for agenda setting vary greatly depending upon the receptiveness of the White House or the Congress to new initiatives. Thus, while the representatives of subnational governments and the functional specialists play a steady role in problem definition, the focus of activity for agenda setting shifts as political officials, institutions, and attitudes change.

This chapter examines problem definition regarding grants programs to determine the ways in which general problems become issues. It then examines agenda setting itself—the process of selecting the issues to which government responds, and the actors and strategies involved in the process at this stage.

may lead to more information about the costs and effects of specific grant programs. In fiscal years 1980 and 1981, grants to states and local governments, which often are controllable, were reduced to help finance direct payments to individuals—the more politically popular programs that account for a major portion of the uncontrollable budget.

INFLUENCES ON THE CONGRESSIONAL PROCESS

Group Organization and Strategies

The lobbyists who are most influential during the congressional phase of the intergovernmental grants process often represent the same interests (and may be the same people) as the lobbyists who attempt to influence the agenda setters. The difference during the congressional decisionmaking stage is that the concept that is being considered may actually become law; lobbyists at the agenda setting stage are occupied solely with problem definition and proposed solutions. During the congressional decisionmaking stage more actors will become involved in the grants process.

There are numerous mechanisms that representatives of the different interest groups use in attempting to influence policy. The formal methods include providing detailed background materials to senators and representatives and presenting testimony at congressional hearings. In addition to bringing problems and fresh ideas into the congressional system, lobbyists often provide technical assistance in drafting new laws and in developing rationales for existing laws. Since 1965, the National Education Association has provided continuing assistance in developing proposals for the various reauthorizations of the Elementary and Secondary Education Act. Similarly, adjustments in revenue sharing formulas would not be of central concern if the representatives of the subnational jurisdictions and public interest groups had not pressed for revisions to the formula for distributing federal funds.

An interesting example of the way in which urban jurisdictions lobbied for changes in a law occurred prior to the passage of the Urban Mass Transportation Act of 1964. Until this bill was enacted, the federal government's transportation assistance was directed almost exclusively toward the construction and maintenance of highways. Furthermore, until 1944 this highway money tended to exclude urban jurisdictions from receiving federal dollars for highway projects. As demands within urban areas developed for more extensive, and often more costly, mass transit systems, city officials started to mobilize. They sent representatives to Washington to lobby for new mass transportation legislation—to be funded from highway revenues. The urban

PROBLEM DEFINITION

What is Problem Definition?

Problem definition is the stage in the evolution of public policy in which opinion leaders define problems and generate ideas.[1] Much of this activity takes place outside of the formal councils of government—in universities, in think-tanks, in interest groups, in the press, and elsewhere.[2] Often government decisionmakers participate in this pre-decisionmaking stage, but not every potential problem becomes an issue for government action. As Charles Lindblom of Yale University notes, "Policy makers are not faced with a *given* problem."[3] Something has to happen to give shape to a set of conditions, and to help policymakers define the problem. It is during this pre-policymaking stage that public consciousness is raised; as policymakers learn about a problem, a *definition of the problem* emerges—along with multiple solutions. Additional debate may be generated, with positions on all sides of the emerging policy issue receiving attention. As this process develops momentum, the president, White House advisors, members of Congress and their staffs, and program managers in the bureaucracy become aware of the issues being raised.

Consider the case of environmental policy. During the late 1960s there was rising public concern over the deteriorating state of the environment—overpopulation, pollution, and depletion of resources. Initially, only a few isolated groups expressed interest in this policy area. The Sierra Club, the Wilderness Society, the Audubon Society, and other environmental groups pushed for action on environmental, conservation, and preservation issues. Increasingly, magazine articles and books such as Rachel Carson's *Silent Spring* advanced the cause of environmental protection. Public concern over this issue increased dramatically in the late 1960s, and environmental disasters such as the Santa Barbara oil spill of 1969 reinforced this growing concern over the pollution question. In 1970, Democratic Senator Gaylord Nelson from Wisconsin sponsored Earth Day legislation, and millions of Americans turned out for clean-up campaigns and rallies on college campuses, in small towns, and in cities.

By 1970, this increasing momentum resulted in the creation of the Environmental Protection Agency (EPA). Congress then enacted the National Environmental Policy Act, the Clean Air Act and, in 1972, the Federal Water Pollution Control Act. Indeed, the enormous public and media interest in the issue created a context in which legislative proposals quickly surfaced and attracted wide attention.

This legislation expanded the federal government's enforcement powers to clean up the nation's air and waterways as well as to provide for expanded state planning and implementation grants.[4] In this policy area the public and media attention sparked the creation of new interest groups and eventual legislative action.

In many cases, problems not defined by a dramatic crisis or by sudden journalistic attention are defined by established public and private interest groups. During the 1960s and 1970s there was increased pressure on the federal government to finance a large share of the costs of income maintenance and services to the poor. This pressure increased despite the lack of presidential support for nationalizing public welfare in the 1950s and 1960s. Arthur Flemming, secretary of the Department of Health, Education, and Welfare during the Eisenhower administration, testified that: "We assume it is possible for the states to participate to a greater extent in the public assistance program than is now the case." And President Eisenhower noted " . . . the State and local responsibility in these programs should be strengthened, not weakened."[5]

State and local officials, however, found it increasingly difficult to provide the funding necessary to maintain adequate public welfare programs. During the early 1960s elected officials and social service professionals began to support greater national involvement in the provision of public welfare. In 1965 Walter Bentrup observed that: "The public income maintenance program of the future must be strictly a federal program. Only the federal government can reach across the length and breadth of the country, uniformly, to assure a decent standard of assistance for all."[6]

In 1969 President Nixon appointed as his domestic policy advisor Daniel Patrick Moynihan, a strong supporter of a national family policy. Moynihan became the prime force behind Nixon's Family Assistance Program (FAP), which was sent to Congress in 1969. Later that year, the National Governors' Conference called for a federally financed system of welfare payments to replace the current federal-state program. In 1971, the National League of Cities declared that: "Welfare in America has become a national problem that requires national solutions."[7]

In 1972, in response both to President Nixon's recommendation for a Family Assistance Program and to the financial presures on states and localities, Congress enacted the Supplemental Security Income Program (SSI). SSI was a partial response to the cost problems afflicting the state and local jurisdictions. It increased the role of federal funding for the needy who are blind, disabled, and aged by establishing a national program to reduce state responsibility for providing welfare assistance.

Who Defines the Problem?

The question of who defines the problem goes to the heart of the policy process; those who define problems set the parameters or boundaries of the politically feasible alternatives. As we have seen, events, the media, and public opinion may force a definition of issues, as in the case of environmental policy. In other instances, such as nationalized welfare funding, professional groups and officials below the national level define issues for national attention. Eventually, it is the president, Congress, and bureaucrats who define the problems more precisely and select the alternatives to be considered.

Individuals and groups will try to influence these formal decisionmakers. While group access to these decisionmakers is unequally distributed, in the last 10 or 15 years numerous, newly organized groups—women, consumers, environmentalists, and new intergovernmental groups such as suburban counties and small towns—have moved into positions of influence alongside older, more established interest groups.

Who, then, influences the "problem definers" in national politics? Generally, it is people who have access to the decisionmakers at this stage in the political process—especially to the president and Congress. The groups change from policy area to policy area though there are some overlapping memberships. The American Medical Association and its state and local affiliates define issues in the area of health care delivery, but they have little impact on defense policy. Similarly, the U.S. Conference of Mayors helps to define urban problems, but not American maritime policy. Although different public policy areas have different sets of problem definers, access is *potentially* open to any individual or group that can sustain the momentum necessary for continuing participation in the political process.[8]

THE ACTORS

Although the range of actors involved in problem definition and agenda setting varies from policy area to policy area, some are involved in numerous issues. The president and Congress will be influenced by different groups and advisers depending upon the issue in question. Some members of Congress are more influential than others in particular policy areas. Thus, if one is concerned with the increasing role of the states in the matter of grants management, the chairman of the Senate Subcommittee on Intergovernmental Relations is an important person. On issues involving grants for housing and community development, the chairman of the Senate Committee on Banking and Urban Affairs plays a prominent role.

There are several sets of central participants in the setting of intergovernmental policy agendas. These participants can be divided into four general categories: 1) national policymakers; 2) state, county, and local officials; 3) functional specialists; and 4) private interest groups.

National Policymakers

Athough numerous groups participate in the process that has created the approximately 500 different grants programs, the president and the White House staff play especially important roles in this process. Though it is easy to overestimate the president's influence, the president's endorsement can give a program a significant boost. The concept of revenue sharing dates back to the 1950s and early 1960s, but it was not until President Nixon endorsed the idea that Congress acted. Actually the president and White House staff are more likely to adopt ideas presented by others than they are to formulate new proposals themselves. Indeed, much of the president's legislative program is routinely generated by policy staffs in the executive agencies.

Within the executive branch, the president's budget advisers and domestic policy staff play important roles early in the decisionmaking process. Before the president discusses policy alternatives or presents a legislative proposal to Congress, a price tag for the proposal must be established by the Office of Management and Budget (OMB). The White House Domestic Policy staff oversees the preparation of bills in executive agencies and resolves conflicts between proposals by various agencies. During the Carter administration, Stuart E. Eizenstat, Carter's chief domestic policy adviser, directed a professional staff of 27 that played a central position in the formulation of legislation. Although Eizenstat frequently went to Capitol Hill to brief legislators about administration proposals, the actual lobbying was usually done by other members of the White House staff. Despite the efforts of OMB and the domestic policy staff, not all conflicts among departments are resolved, and not every agency proposal can be reviewed in depth. Individual agencies also maintain independent working relationships with individual members of Congress. As a result, many proposals may gain legislative backing without White House endorsement.[9]

The increasingly complicated maze of intergovernmental grants encouraged the Carter administration to divide the responsibility for handling intergovernmental relations. In addition to Eizenstat's domestic policy staff, Carter created the Office of the Assistant to the President for Intergovernmental Relations. Jack H. Watson was the head of that office from 1977 to the summer of 1980, when he was promoted to the position of White House Chief of Staff. Watson's small intergovernmental relations staff focused its attention on securing suggestions from state and local groups as well as on monitoring program implementation. While Eizenstat's staff was involved in predecision policy formulation, Watson's intergovernmental relations office was in charge of implementation and problem identification once a policy was in effect.

President Carter took several other steps to open communications between federal, state, and local agencies. He insisted that an influential, high level official in each department and agency be assigned responsibility for intergovernmental relations to enhance the access of state, county, and local officials to national policymakers. Carter also directed all cabinet officers to consult with state and local officials before sending any new budget proposals, reorganization plans, or policy initiatives to him.

Carter's actions demonstrated a more systematic effort to involve state and local officials in policy formulation than had any of his predecessors. As a result, state and local interest groups raised their expectations about the degree to which the White House would consult them. Although Jack Watson continued to receive praise from subnational officials for his role as a policy coordinator, their participation in the policymaking process actually decreased during the Carter administration's final year. It may be that presidents tend to lose interest in intergovernmental relations as they become embroiled in foreign policy.[10] But it may require a more sophisticated explanation than this. Because intergovernmental relations is a complex web of relationships, it is difficult for the president to provide a clear focus on numerous domestic issues, which are often viewed as management problems.

The president's role in the policymaking process varies with the administration's success in bringing about legislative programs. In all cases, however, a public discussion of the issues by the president, by definition, makes issues relevant and places them on the nation's policy agenda.[11] Some presidents have had more success in their relations with Congress than others.

Congress does not act as a rubber stamp for presidential proposals. Indeed, there is a danger of overstating the president's admittedly important role in the agenda-setting process because the president automatically plays a role in policy formulation. The State of the Union Address, the annual budget, and reports to Congress all attract a good deal of media attention. However, often the president is merely endorsing an idea that originated during little-noticed work by an interest group or by a member of Congress. Cynthia Cates Colella of the ACIR explains that, "even passing White House interest may imbue a potential program—initiated in Congress or elsewhere—with enough added importance or salience to aid in its passage.''[12]

In fact, one ACIR study finds that of five policy actors—Congress, the president, interest groups, bureaucrats, and the courts—only Congress consistently has played an important role in policy initiation. Indeed, individual members of Congress and their staffs often act as entrepreneurs, as promoters for a program. The ACIR study notes, "no actor was more vividly responsible in the long run for principal portions of policy initiation than the Congressional activist.''[13]

State and Local Elected Officials

Given the inability of subnational jurisdictions to generate revenues sufficient to meet their service needs, the elected officials and their generalist aides—city managers, planners, and budget directors—try to influence the president and Congress to place additional funding for their unit of jurisdiction and/or for their priority issues on the policy agenda. It is the issue-by-issue focus of these officials that often generates the patchwork quilt effect of federal grants. A federal takeover of the Aid to Families with Dependent Children (AFDC) program (a public assistance program) is a continuing favorite ploy of mayors, county executives, and governors who are striving to balance their budgets. This strategy is of continuing interest since many of these jurisdictions pay a portion of the costs of AFDC. Because the "fiscal bite" is large and relatively uncontrollable, these governments feel that other program needs cannot be met adequately. Also, there have been instances when officials of subnational governments have requested specific "bail-out" funding. Both city and state officials did this with some success during New York City's initial fiscal crisis in the mid 1970s. In 1978, the mayor of Cleveland, Ohio, made a similar request—though with less success.[14]

As fiscal dependence has increased, more subnational governments have supported lobbyists in Washington to protect their interests.[15] This is, of course, an expensive enterprise, and one that not all jurisdictions can afford. Yet it generally is believed that the federal dollars gained or saved for the client more than offset the lobbyists' cost. Approximately 30 states maintain these offices. Cities and counties that cannot afford their own fulltime representative. in Washington may hire consultants; other jurisdictions may rely almost exclusively on the public interest groups (PIGs) to protect their interests. The individual state or local offices, however, have a somewhat different agenda than do these interest groups. A former assistant director of the National Governors' Conference, James Martin, saw little overlap between the services of the Governors' Conference staff and the separate state offices; a state office serves the interests of a particular state, while the conference serves states generally.[16] States and localities that open Washington offices are better able to present their case personally and in a timely fashion. As the intergovernmental programs administrator for the city of Phoenix, Arizona, has said: "When a city speaks only through big organizations, Congress tends to view it as faceless."[17]

Not only do individual mayors, county executives, and governors help define problems, they also help shape the policy agenda. Organizations such as the National League of Cities, U.S. Conference of Mayors, National Association of Counties, National Conference of State Legislatures, and the National Governors' Association have played this role for some time.[18] Other subnational government lobbying groups have started to proliferate in Washington in recent years. The National Association of Towns and Townships, a well-established group, began its lobbying activities in Washington only in 1976, several years after its members became eligible for general revenue sharing funds. The National Association of Smaller Communities, American Association of Smaller Cities, National Association of Regional Councils, and the National Conference of Black Mayors all organized and opened Washington offices during the 1970s. These groups attempt to influence agenda setting by educating Washington policymakers about their role in our federal system. For example, the National Association of Counties spends a good deal of time and effort educating lawmakers and administrators about the important services urban county governments provide. This is a difficult task because counties in some states have only recently started to provide a wide range of services. Other recent arrivals in Washington—the towns and small cities—also devote a large effort to educating the policy community about their special needs.

Recently, groups such as the Coalition of Northeast Governors, Southern Growth Policies Board, and Western Governors Conference have formed to promote regional concerns. The northeastern and midwestern officials are banding together to call attention to what they claim is an imbalance in federal spending favoring the West and South. To counter this attack, southern officials have banded together to protect their share. Not to be outdone, western governors are calling the issues of water rights and state control over energy development to Washington's attention.

Over the past decade the public interest groups have gained ground in the agenda-setting process. During the Nixon-Ford years there were isolated instances of state and local involvement in executive branch preparation of intergovernmental legislation. The PIGs played a role in writing the revenue sharing legislation enacted in 1972, but in 1971 had been shut out of preparation of the legislation to create new block grants. In 1974, officials in the Department of Health, Education, and Welfare invited state officials to help them write a legislative proposal to change the federal regulation of social services. In March 1975, Washington representatives of state and local officials were invited to assist the Office of Management and Budget, at an early stage, to help draft legislation to consolidate 59 programs into four new block grant programs. Although the proposals were never enacted by Congress, the public interest groups took the effort seriously.[19] During the Carter administration this access was continued; in 1977 and 1978, when the administration was developing a national urban policy, many of the groups of subnational officials were consulted.

Functional Specialists

In addition to the attempts of elected state and local officials to influence policy origination, we also find that program specialists—social workers, police chiefs, educators, housing administrators, and others—play important roles in policy development. These officials form their own organizations that actively monitor and seek to influence the workings of congressional subcommittees and administrative agencies.

Only a few of these groups have the political clout to influence the president directly. On the other hand, the specialized nature of their interest and the fact that they are sources of substantive expertise guarantees their access to individual members of Congress as well as to other federal officials. The less visible and smaller programs that do not interest governors or mayors often find program specialists as the primary state or local advocates. In fact, the role of the program officials grows as we move through the policy process. Once a concept is accepted and Congress debates the details of a categorical grant and most block grants, the specialists supersede the generalists. During policy implementation and later efforts to expand and modify the categorical and block grant programs, the relationships between these interest groups, administrative agencies, and legislative staffers come to the foreground.

Private Interest Groups

Not only do public officials define problems and influence federal agenda setters, so too do the private interest groups. The techniques that these groups employ are not unlike those used by public sector officials and organizations. In fact, much of the technique developed by public officials was learned from private sector activity. Representatives of private interests have been long associated with lobbying public officials. Their successes are variable, dependent upon their success in gaining access to the public decisionmakers. As we noted earlier in this chapter, private interests were instrumental in setting the tone for discussion of environmental issues in the late 1960s and early 1970s. Similarly, the American Medical Association (AMA) and the insurance industry have been active participants in defining the limits of debate on health care policy. Other examples of private interest groups that play a major role in policymaking as it concerns their field of interest are the National Education Association (NEA) and the nation's major energy producers.

All of the above actors as well as the media play roles in the agenda-setting process even though ultimately it is the formal governmental actors—the president and Congress—who set the public agenda. Furthermore, different sets of actors employ different strategies to reach their goals. It is to these strategies that we now turn our attention.

THE STRATEGIES

There are several strategies that the various actors use when they are involved in efforts to influence public policy agenda setting. These strategies are used by both the public and private actors— although later we will address specifically the public sector in the intergovernmental grants process. The strategies include group formation, group pressure, task force participation, public statements by well-placed and influential public officials, and use of the media. The strategies that are chosen can depend on many factors, such as the nature of the issue, the existence of allies, or the strength of public opinion. Additionally, the nature of presidential leadership, the mood in Congress, or the personal agendas of one or two key legislators can all shape the agenda-setting strategies.

Individual mayors, county executives, and governors often find that their presentations fail to carry enough weight, but associations of such people working together can reach the multiple access points of the national decisionmaking process. These associations can tap the national media. They can use their resources and staff time to reach greater numbers of people who can be made aware and concerned about the problems the associations are trying to define as national issues.

Group formation is one agenda-setting strategy. After the cities and counties increased their Washington lobbying activities in the 1960s and 1970s, for example, the governors felt that it was necessary to reorient the National Governors' Conference from a passive social club to an active lobbying organization. The renamed group, now the National Governor's Association, opened a Washington office in the mid-1970s and has been aggressively pushing for a stronger state role in federal grant programs.

Since these organizations have fulltime offices in the nation's capital, they maintain continuing contacts with other participants in the political process. In January 1979, President Carter presented a bill to Congress targeted at cities in need of fiscal relief. There was some significant congressional opposition to the proposed legislation. According to his aides, however, the president decided to request $250 million of relief because of the strong statements of urgent need made by a group of mayors—representing the U.S. Conference of Mayors—in a meeting held several weeks earlier.[20]

These public interest groups can help to generate media attention as well. Although the mayor of New York City has access to *The New York Times,* and the mayor of Los Angeles has access to *The Los Angeles Times,* and they both have reasonable access to the national network news programs, the mayors of the thousands of smaller cities and towns cannot individually capture national media attention. However, if the National League of Cities, the nation's largest group of municipal officials, issues a statement, it may receive this national coverage. This presentation will reach the president as well as officials who directly influence urban policy decisions in the Office of Management and Budget, the Department of Housing and Urban Development, and elsewhere. Presentations such as newsletters and legislative reports reach the elected and nonelected opinion leaders throughout the country who, in turn, present positions and can generate the support necessary to move issues onto the public policy agenda.

Not only are some newspapers more visible nationally than others, but some newspaper columnists and media commentators have better access to opinion leaders and decisionmakers. An interesting example of this phenomenon arose in the 1960s. On May 21, 1968, CBS television presented "Hunger in America," a special report on the subject of malnutrition and hunger in the United States. From being a marginal problem in the eyes of most Americans and their policymakers, hungry and malnourished people evolved into a new and serious issue. Special private sector committees were convened, a presidential report was prepared, a presidential conference was planned, and new legislation was introduced by the president to Congress. In December 1970, Congress enacted new and far-reaching legislation—the Food Stamp Program—to reduce hunger and malnutrition among America's poor.[21]

The level of interest a president shows in intergovernmental issues can influence the nature of an agenda-setting strategy. If the president is an activist, individuals and groups will seek out opportunities to participate on presidential task forces and commissions. These panels often are criticized because their findings are not always acted upon. Indeed, these information-collecting devices sometimes seem to be part of the game of symbolic politics; one can line a bookshelf with the various commission reports on racial disorders, political assassinations, pornography, and drugs, for which there was no legislative result.[22] However, many of the basic concepts that underly the social legislation enacted during the Johnson administration originated with task force reports. Several programs—the rent supplement program, the Model Cities program enacted in 1966, and Title III of the Elementary and Secondary Education Act of 1965—were the result of presidential task force activity.[23]

Often the nature of the times can influence agenda-setting strategies. The desire to obtain new federal programs originally was the reason for opening state and local lobbying offices in Washington. After passage of California's Proposition 13 in 1978, and with the interest in balancing the budget in the early 1980s, state and local governments slowed down their quest for new programs and new project grants. Jurisdictions sought to retain what they had or increase their jurisdiction's share of the total by concentrating on existing formulas that allocated federal funds. One state official put it this way: "Obviously if you change a formula, it makes the difference of tens if not hundreds of millions of dollars. If I spent every morning, noon and night on [project] grants, I couldn't make up that money." [24]

Several sets of conditions affect the strategies that will be most useful in influencing problem definers and agenda setters. Presidential style, policy preferences, relations with congressional leaders, and staffing patterns can influence the legislative process. Consider the style and policy preferences of presidents Johnson, Nixon, Carter, and Reagan. Following President Kennedy's assassination, Lyndon Johnson shepherded numerous pieces of social legislation through Congress. Contributing to passage of these domestic policy proposals were Johnson's progressive social ideology, his close relations with congressional leaders, his aggressive political style, and the desire by many in Congress to enact these programs as a tribute to the late President Kennedy. During Johnson's early years as president there was an important and lasting shift toward the expanded use of federal aid to states and localities.

Richard Nixon provided a somewhat different influence on the agenda-setting process. He did not have Johnson's history of good relations with congressional leaders, and he was forced to work with a Congress controlled by the opposition party. Prior to America's heaviest involvement in the Vietnam War, Johnson was very much a "domestic president." That is, he understood domestic politics, had an activist bent, and wanted to help solve many of the nation's internal problems. He recognized the need to use the federal government to deal with many of the problems that had overwhelmed the states and localities. In contrast, Richard Nixon was more comfortable focusing his attention on foreign policy. He was less aggressive on domestic issues, in part, because he had less interest in social policy than Johnson.

Many of Nixon's intergovernmental proposals aimed at changing the mechanism for distributing federal funds. Often the Nixon administration proposed new programs that were about to be initiated by the Democratic Congress. After 1969, for example, public attitudes shifted dramatically in favor of a stronger federal role and greater financial support of state and local antipollution efforts. Credit for enacting environmental programs became a political plum for which it was worth fighting. President Nixon's proposals can be seen as a case of policy "oneupmanship," where he tried to displace Democratic Senator Edmund Muskie of Maine as the leading politician in the field.[25]

Jimmy Carter initiated a different White House role in the agenda-setting process. President Carter came to Washington as an "outsider" to national politics; he had no experience dealing with members of Congress. Despite the fact that Congress was controlled by Democrats, relations between the president and Congress were never particularly good. Unlike Johnson, Carter had considerable doubts about the expanding role of the federal government into the traditional spheres of state and local concerns. Also, throughout most of his presidency, Carter battled a rising inflation rate while struggling to keep a campaign promise to reduce the federal budget deficit. Carter's ideas for the intergovernmental system focused on three basic concepts: 1) precise targeting of aid to needy communities; 2) using public money to leverage private funds to aid urban and community development; and 3) reducing red tape and paperwork.[26] Like Nixon, Carter proposed few new spending programs. In fact, most of the growth of federal grants during his first two years in office can be traced to congressional initiatives, entitlements, and inflation.

Ronald Reagan is unlikely to be an activist in the area of intergovernmental grants. He is a conservative Republican operating with a split Congress—a Democratic majority in the House of Representatives and a Republican majority in the Senate. In addition, like Carter, he is a Washington "outsider." He favors limiting federal involvement in domestic politics. Based upon his record as governor of California and his campaign remarks, it is likely that greater emphasis will be given to block grants and grants management reform. In the early 1980s neither the president nor the Congress is likely to support major new grant programs.

Given these examples of divergent White House styles, it should be clear that the strategies successful in influencing one president may not be effective with another. When the president is reluctant to propose new programs for either ideological or fiscal reasons, it becomes more important to approach members of Congress directly. Congress continues to play a significant role as a policy originator because recent presidents have failed to demonstrate a sustained interest in intergovernmental program development.

CONCLUSIONS

It is apparent that early and consistent pressure by officials of subnational governments is necessary as they become ever more dependent on the federal government for revenue. Major lobbying efforts have been launched by some jurisdictions competing with private interest groups in making demands on federal government decision-makers. Both the president and Congress can play important roles in originating policy. Depending on the issue and on the political conditions, one or the other may be the primary target of groups who are trying to place issues on the governmental agenda.

The work of functional specialists and state and local generalists during problem definition is filtered through a complex and fragmented process of agenda setting. The entrepreneurial role of individual members of Congress is important during this stage, and presidential endorsement can be critical to program success. However, since the era of Great Society legislation in the Johnson administration, presidents have played a less active role, choosing instead to endorse programs initiated by individual members of Congress. This inability or unwillingness of recent presidents to focus their attention on the grants system has contributed to the fragmenting of the process. Hence, the agenda is set not in a comprehensive manner but in a piecemeal fashion, the product of the differential access of the actors and the opportunistic strategies they use.

At the agenda-setting stage of the policy process there are opportunities available for the regulated—states and localities and their functional departments—to influence the processes—laws and regulations—that ultimately will support and regulate their activities. Thus at the very outset of the intergovernmental policy process the interactive negotiation that characterizes regulatory politics seems to be in place.

NOTES

1. See Charles O. Jones, *An Introduction to the Study of Public Policy* (North Scituate, Mass.: Duxbury Press, 1977) for an overview of the policy process.
2. For a review of agenda-setting strategies, see Roger W. Cobb and Charles O. Elder, *Participation in American Politics: The Dynamics of Agenda-Building* (Boston: Allyn & Bacon, 1972), p. 85.
3. Charles E. Lindblom, *The Policy-Making Process* (Englewood Cliffs, N.J.: Prentice-Hall, 1968), p. 13.
4. Charles O. Jones, *Clean Air: The Policies and Politics of Pollution Control* (Pittsburgh: University of Pittsburgh Press, 1975), pp. 175-210.
5. U.S, Senate, Committee on Finance, *Social Security,* 85th Cong., 2d sess., 1958, p. 130.
6. Walter Bentrup, "What's Wrong With the Means Test," *Public Welfare* 23 (October 1965): 238.
7. Gilbert Steiner, *The State of Welfare* (Washington, D.C.: Brookings Institution, 1971), p. 333; and "Our Nation's Obligations to its Cities," *Nation's Cities* 9 (March 1971): 12.
8. Joyce Gelb and Marian Lief Palley, "Women and Interest Group Politics: A Comparative Analysis of Federal Decision Making," *Journal of Politics* 41 (May 1979): 363-364.
9. Larry Light, "White House Domestic Policy Staff Plays an Important Role in Formulating Legislation," *Congressional Quarterly Weekly Report* 37 (October 6, 1979): 2199-2204.
10. Congressional Quarterly, *Spring 1978 Guide to Current American Government* (Washington, D.C.: Congressional Quarterly, 1977), pp. 39-40.
11. William J. Keefe and Morris S. Ogul, *The American Legislative Process* (Englewood Cliffs, N.J.: Prentice-Hall, 1977), p. 170; and Stephen J. Wayne, *The Legislative Presidency* (New York: Harper & Row, Publishers, 1978), pp. 168-173.
12. Cynthia Cates Colella, "The Creation, Care and Feeding of Leviathan: Who and What Makes Government Grow," *Intergovernmental Perspective* 5 (Fall 1979): 8.
13. Ibid., p. 7.
14. *Washington Post,* December 21, 1978.
15. For a good discussion of subnational lobbying in Washington, see Donald Haider, *When Governments Come to Washington* (New York: Free Press, 1974).
16. John L. Moore, "Washington Pressures/State-Local Lobbying Grows Despite Drive to Decentralize Governments," *National Journal* 5 (Feb. 24, 1973): 264.
17. Ibid., p. 269.
18. Rochelle L. Stanfield, "The PIGs: Out of the Sty, Into Lobbying with Style," *National Journal* 8 (Aug. 14, 1976): 1134.
19. Joel Havemann, "Federalism Report/State, Local Officials Help Write Consolidation Plans," *National Journal* 8 (Feb. 21, 1976): 228-233.
20. *New York Times,* Jan. 6, 1979, p. 40.
21. Howard A. Palley and Marian Lief Palley, "A Call for a 'War on Hunger'," *Poverty and Human Resources Abstracts* 7 (September 1972): 316-328.
22. Murray Edelman, *The Symbolic Nature of Politics* (Urbana, Ill.: University of Illinois Press, 1967), p. 16. The term "symbolic politics" is being

used to express the notion that ritual and myth permeate our political institutions and that "symbolic participation is our lot much of the time."

23. Norman C. Thomas and Harold L. Wolman, "The Presidency and Policy Formulation: The Use of Task Forces," *Public Administration Review* 29 (September/October 1969): 459-471.
24. Lisa B. Belkin, "For State and Local Governments Washington is the Place to Be," *National Journal* 12 (September 9, 1980): 1485-1487.
25. Charles O. Jones, "Speculative Argumentation in Federal Air Pollution Policy-Making," *Journal of Politics* 36 (May 1974): 438-464.
26. Rochelle L. Stanfield, "Is the Man from Georgia Ready to Help the States and Cities?" *National Journal* 9 (January 22, 1977): 137.

4

Policy Adoption

Once a problem or an issue has captured the attention of the policymakers, it is the role of Congress to transform the idea into legislation. The president and various interest groups attempt to influence the content of that legislation, but ultimately it is the members of Congress who must pass the laws and devise the formulas to allocate federal funds.

In this chapter we will show that policy adoption is a complex process. As it relates to the grants process, policy adoption is a piecemeal, pluralistic process of combining and balancing national and subnational goals along with general and special interests; it rarely produces comprehensive solutions to problems. Congress tends to distribute benefits broadly and to support conflicting programs. The end result is a haphazard and fragmented grants system in which federal officials cannot always maintain tight regulatory control over state and local program implementation.

We will look first at the fragmenting effects of the congressional system on the grants process. The multiple influences on members of Congress, and the nature of responses to these influences, are examined to demonstrate that the regulated interests are often in a position to influence the regulating interests—at a relatively early stage in the grants policy process.

THE CONGRESSIONAL ACTORS

Several concentrations of power and influence must be examined in the congressional system when we attempt to disentangle the in-

49

tergovernmental grants process. The operations of congressional committees and their personal staffs in both the Senate and the House of Representatives must be understood. In addition, we must recognize the roles of both the congressional budget committees and the Congressional Budget Office (CBO), as well as the nature and scope of the policy areas affected by the intergovernmental grants process. Finally, the noncongressional cast of actors who try to influence the decisionmakers in Congress must be tracked—people working in the White House, in the national bureaucracy, in the state and local bureaucracies, in interest groups representing subnational governments, and in other interest groups representing the specific public and/or private interests of groups in society.

Committees

No one committee or set of committees has total or even near total control over the nature or scope of intergovernmental grants. Rather, for each policy area there are authorization and appropriations committees operating in both houses of Congress. There were five block grants in place for fiscal year 1980, for example. These block grants were considered by five separate authorization committees (and their appropriate subcommittees) in the Senate and an additional five authorization committees in the House of Representatives. In addition to this, the Appropriations Committee in each chamber of Congress had to approve spending limits for these programs; and in each Appropriations Committee separate subcommittees were charged with making the preliminary decisions on appropriation levels. Thus two appropriations committees and ten subcommittees were involved at this stage of the decisionmaking process. In total, twelve congressional subcommittees, and twenty subcommittees, determined the nature and scope of the five block grants that went to subnational jurisdictions. In addition to these five block grants there are also many categorical grants providing aid to subnational governments. Subsequently, many additional committees and subcommittees become involved in the intergovernmental grants decisionmaking process. In 1980 there were more than 100 Senate subcommittees and more than 150 subcommittees functioning in the House of Representatives.

The range of domestic policy concerns that is affected by the intergovernmental grants process is considerable. Intergovernmental grants are provided to state and local jurisdictions for a wide variety of programs to provide education, health and welfare services, environmental services, highways, and transportation services, to name just a few of the major program areas. Table 4-1 illustrates the variety of grant programs in effect in FY 1978. Each of these policy areas is reviewed by a specific set of committees. Given the wide

Table 4-1. Categorical Grants Programs, by Grant Type and Administering Agency: Fiscal Year 1978.

Department or Agency	1978 Total Number	1978 Total Percent	Formula Number	Formula Percent	Project Number	Project Percent
Agriculture	42	8.4	22	12.9	20	6.2
Appalachian Regional Commission	14	2.9	—	—	14	4.3
Commerce	28	5.7	5	2.9	23	7.1
Energy	6	1.2	3	1.8	3	0.9
Environmental Protection Agency	35	7.1	10	5.9	25	7.8
Health, Education and Welfare						
Office of Secretary	2	0.4	1	0.6	1	0.3
Education	96	19.6	39	22.9	57	17.7
Health Care Financing Administration	3	0.6	2	1.2	1	0.3
Human Development Services	40	8.1	13	7.6	27	8.4
Public Health Services	69	14.1	7	4.1	62	19.3
Social and Rehabilitation Service	—	—	—	—	—	—
Social Security Administration	10	2.0	5	2.9	5	1.6
Housing and Urban Development	14	2.9	—	—	14	4.3
Interior	19	3.9	8	4.7	11	3.4
Justice	13	2.6	3	1.8	10	3.1
Labor	22	4.5	13	7.6	9	2.8
Transportation	50	10.2	29	17.1	21	6.5
Other[a]	29	5.9	10	5.9	19	5.9
Totals	492	100.1	170	99.9	322	99.9

[a] Includes ACTION, Civil Service Commission, Community Services Administration, Department of Defense, General Services Administration, National Foundation for Arts and Humanities, National Institutes of Health, National Science Foundation, Small Business Administration, Veterans Administration, and Water Resources Council.

SOURCE: *A Catalog of Federal Grant-In-Aid Programs to State and Local Governments: Grants Funded FY 1978* (Washington, D.C.: Advisory Commission on Intergovernmental Relations, 1979), p. 5.

range of committees involved, it is difficult to generalize about the operations of the intergovernmental grants process in Congress. Moreover, the proliferation of subcommittees in the Congress indicates that leadership roles have been spread to so many legislators that there is no longer an easily identifiable set of leaders.

The Congressional Budget Process

Congress enacted the Congressional Budget and Impoundment Control Act in 1974. Several major changes were brought about by this law. In particular, although "the reorganization is simply an overlay upon the old budgetary process, . . . most Congressional institutions have been influenced by the reform." [1] The act established congressional budget committees, the Congressional Budget Office (CBO), a new set of budgetary procedures, a budget timetable, a change in the fiscal year, standardized budget terminology, and new procedures for controlling presidential impoundments. [2]

Congress sets budget constraints for itself based on the guidelines proposed by the Congressional Budget Committee, and ideally it should stay within these limits. This procedure has been in place since fiscal 1975, however, and it is clear that federal spending has not been contained.

Many of the grants to subnational governments are uncontrollable because they are based upon specific requirements written into law. Grants to states for Aid to Families with Dependent Children cannot be limited under existing law. The federal government must reimburse the states a specific amount, which is determined by the number of eligible recipients. Grants for Medicaid also cannot be capped. However, funds for social services to welfare recipients provided under Title XX of the Social Security Act *are* limited; in FY 1980 the funding level was $3.1 billion. [3] In fact, of the $199.4 billion appropriation for HEW in fiscal 1980, $177.8 billion was accounted for by entitlements. Entitlements allow eligible individuals to receive transfer payments automatically, based on statutory provisions. In other words, almost 90 percent of the HEW budget—representing 37.5 percent of the federal budget—was uncontrollable due to entitlements, and fed by rising inflation rates. [4]

The CBO provides Congress with budgetary information and analysis. As a result, Office of Management and Budget (OMB) and executive department reports are no longer the only sources of federal budgetary data and analysis. From the vantage point of the intergovernmental grants process this relatively new budget system may have the effect of balancing inputs into the decisionmaking system. The creation of the CBO and the congressional budget committees

lobbyists' success was partially due to coalition with suburban legislators. The Urban Mass Transportation Act of 1970 authorized $3.1 billion in aid to local mass transit systems over a five-year time period. While these funds were limited to loans for investments, capital grants, and demonstration projects, passage of the law marked an important breakthrough for mass transportation. The Federal Aid-Highway Act of 1973 expanded urban mass transit programs further, allowing local jurisdictions to divert Highway Trust Fund revenues to mass transit systems. This mechanism was strengthened by the passage of the National Mass Transportation Act of 1974. Beginning in 1976, all federal funds for mass transit were required to come entirely from the Highway Trust Fund rather than from general revenue sources. This major change in policy, a very real success for the urban lobbyists, changed the decades-old policy that revenues from gasoline taxes could finance highways only.[5]

It would be a mistake to assume that pressures on Congress come solely from private or public interest groups. The administration and the federal bureaucracy actively lobby members of Congress and their staffs, just as members of Congress lobby each other. The president maintains a congressional liaison office, as do the major departments and agencies of the bureaucracy. People working in these units attempt to influence Congress to enact favorable legislation. Furthermore, highly visible public officials, such as departmental secretaries and agency directors, spend a large part of their time lobbying Congress. Their most visible efforts take the form of public testimony before congressional committees.

The National and Subnational Interests

The idea of a single national interest is a very difficult concept to define even in terms of only one policy area. Intergovernmental grants encompass multiple policy areas, and therefore the notion of national interest is an even more unwieldly concept. Similarly, the interests of subnational governments often differ, and they vary from policy area to policy area or from region to region.

In general, it is in the interests of the subnational governments to support those federal grants that provide the most money for the lowest matching requirement and fewest regulations attached to receipt of funds. It is in the national interest to maintain limits on the flow of federal dollars to subnational governments so that federal fiscal control is maintained. It is also in the national interest to insure that certain guidelines are followed by grant recipients. Since the budget of the United States is a statement of national policy, a broader perspective on policy and programs is maintained by the national decisionmakers. Conversely, because officials of the states and localities want federal dollars to help maintain their programs at the least possible local cost to their citizens, they seek increased federal aid. Members of Congress, as officials of a national government, and as representatives of subnational governments, must balance these conflicting demands.

Consider the case of the budget debate during 1980. In an effort to contain the expenditures of the federal government, suggestions were made during the budget debate to reduce funding for several programs that provide assistance to subnational governments. Some members of Congress argued that, given the budget surpluses most states had in both 1978 and 1979, the states and localities should be able to continue their programs with a smaller flow of federal dollars. The fact that many of the voters appeared to prefer restrained public spending—as demonstrated in passage of Proposition 13 in California and restrictions in other states—reinforced this view. Additionally, the action of many states in supporting the call for a constitutional convention to consider amending the Constitution to require a balanced federal budget sparked a move to drop the states' allocation for revenue sharing that year.

Of course, many expensive programs—such as Medicaid and Aid to Families with Dependent Children—are not affected by these cuts. Several popular programs were attacked by the budget cutters, however. For example, in its proposed budget the administration cut 158,000 of the 358,000 public service jobs for adults (plus 228,700 jobs for teenagers) from the general countercyclical (antirecession) public service employment program. The Comprehensive Employment and Training Act (CETA) budget was scheduled to be reduced by a total of $535 million.[6]

The responses to these proposed reductions were varied. Organized labor, city leaders, and several PIGs protested the budget cuts. The U.S. Conference of Mayors issued a statement in which it declared that the proposed reductions in funding for CETA would serve to increase unemployment. Speaker of the House Thomas P. O'Neill, Jr. of Massachusetts told reporters that he had "not become Speaker of the House to dismantle the programs that I've worked all my life for."[7] Gregory Wurzburg, director of the National Council on Employment Policy noted that "public service jobs are vulnerable on the Hill. I don't think you'll see any additions."[8] Secretary of Labor F. Ray Marshall presented a broader perspective by responding within the context of national policy. He noted that "while I strongly believe in the value of the public service jobs, we must never forget that five out of six jobs in our economy are in the private sector. It was very important to put more emphasis on private sector activity and less on public employment."[9]

Consider again the members of Congress who must decide whether to maintain CETA expenditures. The member representing an area with high unemployment levels may be very wary of voting to reduce expenditure levels for this program. On the other hand, in 1979 and 1980 the budget cutting and balancing issue gained strength in Washington. Two possible voting strategies are available to legislators: voting in support of district interests and needs, or voting based on a vague concept of a national public interest. Here multiple pressures, which have been operating throughout the budgetary process, will be brought to bear on congressional voting. Members of Congress who perceive that CETA funding is an important issue in their district may follow constituent sentiment. If the issue is not thought to be significant to constituent interests, then it will be easier for the legislator's vote to reflect a broader conception of national interest— in this case, the need for reduced government spending.

On the one hand, state and local elected and administrative officials may be making demands on their representatives and senators to support programs that provide them with fiscal assistance. Public interest groups reinforce these demands in a broader, often more sophisticated, manner. On the other hand, the administration may be articulating policy alternatives within a broader national context, which may in fact be at variance with state and local needs.

The Role of Elected Officials

Just as national decisionmakers differ in perspectives from state and local officials, so too do the various subnational decisionmakers differ among themselves. More specifically, there are *constituency generalists* (elected officials and their staffs) and *program specialists,* both of whom make demands on the national decisionmakers.

Consider first the elected officials—aided by nonelected generalist managers such as city managers and budget directors—and the pressures they bring to bear on congressional decisionmakers. The mayor of a large city may try to influence the representative from the district in which the city is located to support increased allocations for urban areas. Most often, these pressures are directed toward general fiscal relief rather than the more specific components of a program. In fact, the elected officials of general purpose subnational governments have been very active in their support of broad-based programs— specifically general revenue sharing and block grants.

Members of Congress are interested in reelection and so will pay attention to officials from their home districts. These officials often have access to the local media and can, therefore, easily reach the local voters. In so doing, they provide cues for their constituents.

Today, more than 30 states and approximately 100 cities maintain offices in Washington, D.C. These operations serve several functions for their jurisdictions. A lobbyist can maintain a daily presence in Washington and an ongoing vigil over proposed legislation. The liaison personnel can lobby the district representative and the senators from their state. When appropriate, an elected or administrative official from the jurisdiction can be informed of the need to call or be present to try to influence their elected representatives on legislation being considered. These liaison offices perform other nonlobbying functions, such as keeping track of available grants and monitoring both formula and regulation changes.

This kind of lobbying has proven beneficial in many instances. Louis DeMars, president of the Minneapolis city council, expressed the belief that an all-out lobbying effort helped his city retain $6 million in CETA money for fiscal 1979. Although Minneapolis had experienced a considerable decline in unemployment in the years just prior to fiscal 1979, it was evident that job losses were on the horizon if the proposals for changing the CETA formula were adopted. The city actively lobbied its congressional representatives, "letting them know which provisions of both the House and Senate bills benefited and which ones hurt the city." In addition, DeMars noted that they supported their own stance "by identifying other cities on which the legislation would have basically the same impact."[10]

Not only do the elected subnational officials lobby their representatives in Congress, but their organizations—such as the U.S. Conference of Mayors and the National Governors Association—maintain ongoing lobbying organizations in Washington. The groups develop strategies to influence the legislative process and also follow congressional proceedings to keep their membership informed. They maintain ongoing lobbying operations in Congress and thus are able to keep members of both Houses aware of the interests of their membership. When specific members of Congress need to be influenced, however, influential people from the members' home districts, rather than fulltime lobbyists from the groups, often will be brought in to do that job.

The fact that these groups represent different jurisdictions often provides a basis for cooperation. For example, the U.S. Conference of Mayors has its strongest support among urban legislators from the Northeast and Midwest; the National Association of Counties' strongest supporters tend to be suburban and Republican legislators. When these groups coordinate their efforts they frequently can develop a broad base of legislative support.

The PIGs also develop general policies that would, if enacted into law, benefit the jurisdictions they represent. These presentations are not directed solely to members of Congress, but also to agenda builders and sometimes the general public. This latter strategy often is employed to inform representatives that a particular problem has a wide range of interest and thus brings pressure to bear on members of Congress to lend support to the public interest groups' concern.

The Role of Program Specialists

The program specialists, like the elected officials, attempt to influence national decisionmakers. It is important to remember, however, that the interests of the two groups do not always converge and may in fact be contradictory. Program specialists actually administer specific programs and may have narrow interests. The number of specialist groups is large, and it is not realistic to cluster them all together. Public welfare officials will have different concerns from administrators of highway programs. Both sets of policy administrators are much more likely to be specific in their demands to national decisionmakers regarding the kinds of intergovernmental assistance they would like than are the constituency generalists.

Program administrators are likely to have ongoing relationships with their counterparts in the national bureaucracy and so may be influential in the initial development of congressional program proposals. State-level administrative officials tend to form interest groups around narrow functional bases. They relate to an agency in Washington, and there is "frequent extensive in-fighting and maneuvering between them." [11] These relationships are central to the picket fence model discussed in Chapter 2. The relationships between federal, state, and local administrators often are stronger than the bonds between generalists and specialists at any level of government.

Martha Derthick has suggested that "when federal and state agencies act cooperatively, they have much protection, individually or together, against unwanted intervention from legislatures at either or both levels of the federal system." [12] Many limited purpose agencies such as housing, water supply, and resource conservation often were created as a result of federal funding and have added to local government fragmentation in both rural and urban areas. This has led to a condition in which elected officials and program managers may work at cross purposes. [13]

Consider the different types of pressure exerted on a member of Congress by the elected official and the specialist. As noted previously, generalists are vocal in their demands for broad, general purpose federal programs such as revenue sharing. In fact, their lobbyists pressured Congress to enact the State and Local Fiscal Assistance Act of 1972. The elected officials and their PIGs maintained solid support for this program throughout the 1970s. This is the case even though the major fiscal relief that urban political leaders had hoped would derive from this program has not been forthcoming.[14] However, during the debate of the 1980 renewal of revenue sharing, the U.S. Conference of Mayors did not oppose the Carter administration's proposals to drop the state share from the program. The only thing that the substate public interest groups could agree on during this debate was the maintenance of the local share of revenue sharing.

Although revenue sharing funds reach the same jurisdictions as categorical aid, the revenue sharing money flows directly into the jurisdiction's coffers and so comes under the control of the constituency generalists. The elected chief executive and the members of the legislative assembly of the jurisdiction can use these funds for whichever programs they choose. Specialists such as state health and welfare administrators, for example, lack direct access to these funds for their programs. If funds are program-specific for health and welfare, then these program administrators will receive the funds. Even if the general revenue sharing funds do flow ultimately to the health and welfare programs, the political strings attached may be different from those associated with the categorical program. Paul Terrell found in his study of human services administrators in California that the program managers view revenue sharing and block grants as ineffective means of redressing urban problems.[15] In fact 68 percent of the program specialists Terrell questioned thought that block grants would "swallow up" valuable programs in the areas of community mental health, health programs, community action programs, welfare, and model cities.[16]

FORMULAS AND THE ISSUE OF DISTRIBUTION

Funding formulas are central to the grants process. Yet the battle over the formula to allocate grant funds takes place only after significant support has been generated for a program. Once this support has been established, the distribution of funds becomes a major issue. Later, when programs are scheduled for reauthorization by Congress, the distribution of funds may be the *primary* issue.

There is no single formula for distributing federal dollars to state and local governments. In fact, in 1977 the ACIR estimated that "the distributive pattern in the aggregate is a product of 146 separate formulas and thousands of project grant awards, rather than any coherent national policy." [17] Thus formula setting becomes an endeavor that affected groups attempt to influence to their benefit. It is necessary to remember that "the formula is merely a tool for performing a very old political balancing act: putting the money where the needs are while making sure that every congressional district gets something. . . . formula elements are chosen politically, and seemingly minor changes can mean boom or bust for some recipients of aid." [18]

The ways in which different formulas affect jurisdictions are illustrated by the case of general revenue sharing.[19] When general revenue sharing became law in 1972, a complex formula for the distribution of federal money was developed by the conference committee seeking to reach a compromise between the Senate and House bills. That formula was based on a jurisdiction's level of taxes, personal income, and population. The tax effort criteria were included to reward localities already providing services, while not rewarding governments that historically did very little. In addition, an alternative five-variable formula was generated for urban areas to obtain additional funds.

Yet not every jurisdiction is happy with the formula. Officials in older, declining cities would like to change the current formula that limits their grants to 145 percent of their county's grant per capita and limits the counties to 145 percent of their state's average grant. In practice, this limits the amount of grants to fiscally troubled cities since their allocation is determined not only by the allocation formula, but also by a fixed percentage of the allocation for the county and state in which they are located. Localities that rely heavily on fees and charges, rather than taxes, for items like sewers want the formula adjusted to include fees, as well as taxes, when their tax effort is computed.

The House Subcommittee on Intergovernmental Relations and Human Resources developed data on the effects of different revenue sharing formulas on the nation's 29 largest cities (excluding Washington, D.C.). The variation in appropriation levels illustrates the importance of lobbying for formula modification. Table 4-2 illustrates the difference a single formula can make. If the per capita ceiling is raised from 145 percent of the county ceiling to 300 percent of the county ceiling, or if fees are included, allocations to individual cities can be altered radically.

In addition to the revenue sharing and block grants programs, two-thirds of the categorical grant funds are distributed by formula. Very often it is to these distribution mechanisms that lobbyists address themselves when legislation is being considered. Indeed, the reliance on sophisticated formulas has created an era of "politics by printout." Members of Congress often refuse to vote until they see detailed district-by-district printouts showing the results of alternate formulas. The search for a better formula actually may be a search for a formula that benefits a legislator's district—and helps enough other districts to ensure support from their elected representatives.

Table 4-2. What a Difference a Formula Makes: Impact of Two Potential Changes In Revenue Sharing *(millions of dollars).*

	1976 Grant 145% Ceiling	With 300% of County Grant Ceiling	Fees Included in Computation of Tax Effort
New York	$253.8	$273.2	$249.5
Chicago	68.5	79.9	66.7
Los Angeles	35.4	42.4	38.0
Philadelphia	50.1	88.3	50.0
Detroit	42.1	53.1	42.1
Houston	18.0	16.2	17.1
Baltimore	26.5	31.3	26.4
Dallas	13.6	13.6	13.5
Cleveland	13.7	17.2	15.2
Indianapolis	12.1	12.0	10.2
Milwaukee	12.8	14.2	13.9
San Francisco	19.4	19.1	20.3
San Antonio	9.6	8.4	10.3
San Diego	6.8	7.0	9.3
Boston	20.8	33.2	20.6
Memphis	11.8	11.8	13.6
St. Louis	14.4	28.2	14.3
New Orleans	18.0	18.7	18.0
Phoenix	9.3	8.7	9.7
Columbus	7.6	8.9	8.6
Seattle	8.7	9.7	10.3
Jacksonville	9.2	9.7	8.6
Pittsburgh	13.4	11.5	13.3
Denver	13.1	13.0	13.6
San Jose	4.8	4.8	5.2
Cincinnati	9.7	12.0	9.8
Atlanta	6.5	7.7	8.0
Kansas City	10.2	10.1	10.1
Nashville-Davidson	8.4	8.6	8.5

SOURCE: U.S., House of Representatives, Government Operations Committee, Subcommittee on Intergovernmental Relations and Human Resources.

The Congressional District

Members of Congress must look to their districts for reelection. They must therefore be responsive to the voters in their districts at least on those issues the voters indicate are important to them. In contrast to earlier eras, political parties no longer provide a strong control over senators and representatives; members of the same political party no longer feel the need to vote together. Often there are factors other than party affiliation that influence congressional voting. Democrats, for example, may tend to vote for increases in fiscal relief to urban areas. However, many Democrats represent urban areas or older suburbs in need of fiscal relief and were elected due to this ideological predisposition to favor such aid.[20] Since party control is weak, members of Congress are able to be relatively responsive to organized groups from their district or state. An example of how pressure is brought to bear is provided by the Community Development Block Grant program.

Community Development Block Grant (CDBG) money is distributed to jurisdictions on the basis of a legislative formula.[21] When the formula for the program was established in 1974, it was based on three factors: poverty, overcrowded housing, and population. This formula, which did not consider the age of the housing stock, favored the newer, southern Sun Belt cities at the expense of the northern Frost Belt cities. In an effort to aid the older, declining northern and midwestern cities, Congress in 1977 added an alternate formula that emphasized stock of pre-1940 housing. This formula favored the older eastern cities. Because the total size of the federal aid pie increased, no Sun Belt city lost funding as a result of the alternate formula. In fact, many southern cities actually received more money, although the Sun Belt proportion of the total CDBG funding dropped.

The days of expanding federal revenues are ending, however, and the alternate formula has become a symbol of the Sun Belt's fight for what it deems to be its fair share of the federal aid pie. A variety of groups have attacked this new formula. The Southern Growth Policies Board criticized the measure of pre-1940 housing stock, claiming that it is not really a measure of need. ". . . they wanted to shift the money to the Northeast and they couldn't find any better measure," said David Peterson, director of the group's Washington, D.C., office.[22] Often the distribution of intergovernmental grants generates more controversy than the program goals. Even fiscally conservative legislators will battle for larger shares of federal funds for their state or district.

Constructing Political Coalitions

There are at least two sets of conflicts influencing national decisionmakers when they are considering the nature and scope of intergovernmental grants—conflicts between national and subnational interests, and conflicts between subnational generalists and federal-state-local specialists. The obvious question one must answer is: What kinds of compromises are reached? Given the proliferation of grants and the increase in the funds transferred by the federal government, pork barrel politics have become more prevalent. Of course, this is not just a phenomenon related to decisionmaking in the inter-governmental grants process. It is a broader operating mode that has grown out of the constituency-based interests of members of Congress and the pluralist interests that attempt to influence congressional decisionmaking.

The necessity for compromise is illustrated by the case of the Community Development Block Grants. The economically declining jurisdictions of the North certainly would have received more Community Development Block Grant dollars if the new formula simply had replaced the original formula. But members of Congress representing northern districts knew that if they were unyielding in their support for such a position, a new formula for funds distribution most likely would not be enacted, and their constituents would not receive any additional fiscal relief. So a compromise was reached—a typical tactic in pork barrel politics.

Oftentimes compromises must be drawn not only between regions, but between separate public or private interest groups or between national and subnational interests. States line up against cities and/or counties in the congressional arena, for example. During the past decade the counties and cities have increased their share of federal grants at the expense of the states.[23] More money now flows directly to local jurisdictions than previously was the case, and local governments are winning out in the contest with the states to determine which jurisdictions receive federal aid and which will have their aid cut. Local units of government have the edge perhaps because they outnumber the states, and because there are many more elected local officials than there are state officials. These local officials can bring greater pressure to bear on the federal government in Washington because they are more labor intensive, with a far larger number of employees, and have developed more aggressive lobbying techniques in Washington.

Hartford, Connecticut, is an older northeastern city suffering from high unemployment, a declining tax base, a large number of poor residents, declining neighborhoods, and racial tension. Deputy Mayor Nicholas Carbone has noted that "like many cities, the city of Hartford has made a determined effort to solve the problems within its own borders. But Hartford has gone further: we have made an equally determined effort to have an effect on the federal government's policy towards cities." [24] Thus Hartford, like many similar jurisdictions, has developed a strong local technical staff. They have also established a Washington liaison office and enlisted the support of the city's private sector in lobbying the federal government. Finally, Hartford city officials have been encouraged to take active roles in influencing the White House, Congress and the federal agencies.[25]

The conflicts and ultimate compromises reached among private interest groups and between public and private groups is, of course, the grist of pluralist politics. The case of federal aid for urban mass transit systems discussed earlier in this chapter provides an example of this.[26]

Until the early 1970s, state highway departments had been successful in their efforts to continue expanding the American highway system—due primarily to their lobbyists in Washington and an alliance with rural interests, automobile manufacturers, and oil companies. This coalition successfully maintained a formula for distribution of federal funds that consistently benefited highways. In addition, the Highway Trust Fund until 1973 provided that all revenue in the fund could only be used for highway development, contributing to the "highways only" transportation mentality in the United States Congress. However, local planners, environmentalists, and local officials began to make counter demands on the Congress for the funding of mass transit systems in the 1970s. The National Mass Transportation Act of 1974 provided an $11 billion appropriation for grants and loans to urban mass transit systems, and for the continued substitution of rapid transit projects for segments of interstate highway systems.

Despite these movements away from a highway-focused transportation policy, the highway system is still the dominating force in the competition for federal transportation funds. Compromises regarding appropriations and allocations similar to those discussed above, and interest group politics, continue to be key components of the intergovernmental grants system—with both public and private actors playing roles.

The politics of compromise between national and subnational interests requires separate comment. We have suggested in this chapter that the perspective of overarching national policy may be quite different from the narrower perspective held by subnational officials. While the president and Congress are concerned with overall national budget policy, the chief executive of a city or a county, or a program official in a state or locality, is more concerned with providing daily services to local residents.

In his fiscal 1980 budget, President Carter proposed funding cuts for the impact aid program of assistance to local school districts that provide education to dependents of federal civilian and military personnel. More specifically, he proposed cutting $288 million from the fiscal 1979 allocation of $528 million.[27] He was attempting to contain federal spending and reduce the federal deficit. However, the districts that receive the federal impact aid anticipate that revenue in their overall budget—they are more concerned with their service delivery functions than with an overarching national budget strategy.

In fact, many education officials suggested that the cuts in the federal budget be taken from other programs; program officers of these other agencies could provide similar arguments.

Members of Congress often are hesitant to vote in favor of a national interest if their constituents will suffer at its expense. In this case it was argued that a cut in impact aid would lead to increases in local property taxes—a politically unpopular alternative. One obvious result of this concern is the ever-increasing size of federal budget outlays. Although much of this expansion was *not* controllable, budget outlays increased between 1978 and 1979 by over $50 billion.[28]

There is usually less controversy associated with the renewing and refunding of a program than with the initial funding. Once a program has been established and funded, there are administrative agency demands to retain the program, constituent interest pressure to retain the program, and a "political maintenance system based in no small part on the cooptation and incorporation of Congress itself."[29] In addition, needs are generated by existing programs that make cancelling or reducing them very difficult. Herbert Kaufman made the point well when he noted that:

> Services and programs are instituted because they fill a need not otherwise met, whereupon people begin to count on them and to plan in the light of them. Terminating them would therefore cause hardship and even suffering, the effects of which radiate outward through society. . . . these social costs tip the balance against termination. Government officers dare not ignore them the way private interests can. Governmental activities therefore tend to go on indefinitely.[30]

Cynthia Cates Colella made a corresponding observation when she noted that "In a society which can create a 'need' for Halston blue jeans, any legitimate advantage becomes a necessity, and necessities are seldom relinquished without a struggle."[31]

CONCLUSIONS

Congress responds to a wide variety of actors interested in intergovernmental relations. Executive agencies, private interest groups, state and local leaders and administrators all attempt to influence the legislative process. Congress generally responds to these requests in a piecemeal fashion through its fragmented committee and subcommittee system. As a result, the number of grant programs has grown dramatically in the years since President Johnson's Great Society era. In recent years Congress has been willing to provide for direct grants to a larger and larger number of local governments. This has led to increased conflict over the distribution of funds. The politics of formula creation has led to an era of printout politics, where the distribution of funds at times seems more important than the programmatic purpose.

During the period of expanding programs, the PIGs stressed cooperation and often were united on major issues such as general revenue sharing. Developments during 1979 and 1980 suggest that conflicts may increase as states, cities, and counties each try to hold on to their programs and as the growth in grants slows down and begins to decline. Yet the fragmentation within Congress and the accompanying power of special interest groups and program specialists show no sign of reduced importance. The intergovernmental grants system probably will continue to be modified and added to in the same incremental and haphazard manner as it has in the past, leading to a continued overlap of the regulated and the regulators in the political process.

NOTES

1. John W. Ellwood and James A. Thurber, "Some Implications of the Congressional Budget and Impoundment Control Act for the Senate" (Paper prepared for delivery at the Annual Meeting of the American Political Science Association, Chicago, Ill., Sept. 1-5, 1976), p. 1.
2. Ibid.
3. Elizabeth Wehr and Harrison H. Donnelly, "HEW Gets 'Survival Funding' Despite $200 Billion Budget," *Congressional Quarterly Weekly Report* 37 (January 27, 1979): 131.
4. Ibid., p. 127.
5. U.S., Department of Transportation, Federal Highway Administration, *The 1973 Federal Aid Highway Act, An Analysis* (Washington, D.C.: n.d.), pp. 4-5.
6. Wehr and Donnelly, "HEW Gets 'Survival Funding'," p. 124.
7. Ibid.
8. Ibid.
9. Ibid.
10. Louis G. DeMars, "Lawyer-Lobbyists," *Council Policy Leadership Program—Special Report* (Washington, D.C.: National League of Cities, February 26, 1979), p. 6.
11. Center for Policy Research and Analysis, National Governors' Conference, "The States, Governors, and Policy Management: Changing the Equilibrium of the Federal System," Vol. III, Committee Report. Quoted in Office of Management and Budget, *Strengthening Public Management in the Intergovernmental System* (Washington, D.C.: Executive Office of the President, 1975), p. 12.
12. Martha Derthick, *The Influence of Federal Grants: Public Assistance in Massachusetts* (Cambridge: Harvard University Press, 1970), p. 212.
13. Office of Management and Budget, *Strengthening Public Management*, p. 12.
14. Marian Lief Palley and Howard A. Palley, *Urban America and Public Policies* (Lexington, Mass.: D. C. Heath & Co., 1977), p. 69.

15. Paul Terrell, "Beyond the Categories: Human Service Managers View the New Federal Aid," *Public Administration Review* 40 (January/February 1980): 47-54.
16. Ibid., p. 52.
17. David B. Walker, "Federal Aid and the Federal System," *Intergovernmental Perspective* 3 (Fall 1977): 11.
18. Rochelle L. Stanfield, "Playing Computer Politics with Local Aid Formulas," *National Journal* 10 (December 19, 1978): 1977.
19. Ibid., pp. 1977-1981. This discussion of general revenue sharing formulas relies heavily on Stanfield's article. See also Samuel H. Beer, "The Adoption of General Revenue Sharing," *Public Policy* 24 (1976): 127-195.
20. Joyce Gelb and Marian Lief Palley, *Tradition and Change in American Party Politics* (New York: T. Y. Crowell Co., 1975), pp. 292-293.
21. This discussion of the Community Development Block Grant Program relies heavily on Rochelle L. Stanfield, "Pockets of Poverty—The Other Side of Houston," *National Journal* 11 (March 25, 1979): 476-479.
22. Ibid., p. 479.
23. See Chapter 1 for a discussion of this changing intergovernmental fiscal relationship.
24. Nicholas Carbone, "An All Out Effort," *Council Policy Leadership Program—Special Report* (Washington, D.C.: National League of Cities, February 26, 1979), p. 1.
25. Ibid.
26. Palley and Palley, *Urban America and Public Policies.* Chapter 9 provides a more detailed discussion of the politics of urban mass transit.
27. Wehr and Donnelly, "HEW Gets 'Survival Funding'," p. 130.
28. Christopher R. Conte, "Fiscal 1980 Budget: 'The Policy of Restraint'," *Congressional Quarterly Weekly Report* 37 (January 27, 1979): 110.
29. David A. Stockman, "The Social Pork Barrel," *The Public Interest* 39 (Spring 1975): 13.
30. Herbert Kaufman, *Are Government Organizations Immortal?* (Washington, D.C.: Brookings Institution, 1976), p. 64.
31. Cynthia Cates Colella, "The Creation, Care and Feeding of Leviathan: Who and What Makes Government Grow," *Intergovernmental Perspective* 5 (Fall 1979): 9.

5

The Implementation
of Federal Grants

The role of federal administrators during the implementation of grant programs is very important. Federal laws are often vague; administrators are frequently required to interpret them and to supply the details of implementation. As we have already discussed, the federal grants process is fragmented, and as a result, influence is diffused. Federal agencies need political allies from a wide variety of jurisdictions to help ensure congressional support. So politics plays a part in most transactions, and strict enforcement of grant requirements often is difficult because of the mutually supportive relationship that can develop between officials of the regulating (federal) and the regulated (state and local) governments. Bargaining, compromise, and negotiation are key components of program implementation.

Like other aspects of the policy process, implementation is a highly charged political struggle.[1] The time needed to enact a complex intergovernmental program often is measured in years, not weeks or months. Practical problems of program design and political controversy lead to delays in implementing programs. Bureaucrats play important roles during program development, and later they stand at the center of the volatile implementation process. They play both technical and political roles, by allocating funds, formulating regulations that coordinate programs, and monitoring state and local performance. Bureaucrats do not act alone in performing these tasks. Members of Congress, national interest groups, and state or local officials try to influence their actions.

In this chapter the federal administrative process affecting the politics of federal grants will be examined. More specifically, the grants process will be traced through the federal bureaucracy; questions of administrative discretion, the writing of regulations, and the allocation of grants funds will be discussed. Next the organizational morass of federal administrative agencies will be examined to provide an understanding of the difficulties associated with federal oversight and monitoring of state and local programs funded with federal grants. An understanding of the entanglements that arise in the administrative process will help clarify the nature of the regulatory relationship we have been developing in this volume.

ADMINISTRATIVE DISCRETION

Policy implementation involves conflict. Congress regularly sidesteps controversy as part of the consensus-building effort, so the administrative details of a new law tend to be vague. Legislators cannot master every technical issue or formulate rules governing every application of the law; it is unrealistic to expect the legislative branch to resolve every issue. When groups that are dissatisfied with the outputs of the legislative process reopen old issues during the implementation stage, the result is administrative discretion or the opportunity for bureaucrats to fill in the details of the law.

Policy implementation is much less visible than legislative action, but the bureaucratic struggle still involves a wide range of participants. During implementation fewer members of Congress will intervene in the administrative process—perhaps only subcommittee heads or legislators with specific problems in their district. Also, while mayors and governors are often active lobbyists in Congress, the key actors from the state and local level in the policy implementation process are likely to be program specialists. These changes in the major participants means that many issues are negotiated in more detail or are renegotiated, and no single actor or level of government dominates the process.

Federal actors are the key decisionmakers at the outset of program implementation since they are responsible for allocating funds, writing regulations, and monitoring grants. Yet there are important limits to their influence. One limitation is the need to maintain the support of state and local officials to guarantee a supportive coalition in Congress. Other constraints arise from the scale of intergovernmental policy. The expansion of the grants-in-aid system to include thousands of local governments during the Great Society and New Federalism years makes it impossible for many aid administrators to develop more than a passing acquaintance with grantees. This forces federal officials to develop procedures that they can apply across-the-board, reducing their flexibility to respond to problems in individual jurisdictions. Thus, federal agencies can achieve only imperfect control over recipients.

GUIDELINES AND REGULATIONS

One important way in which laws are translated into concrete programs is in the formulation of administrative guidelines. Guidelines can take many forms. The most formal ones are regulations, governed by requirements for advance publication and opportunities for public comment under the Administrative Procedures Act.

The explosion of legislative action in recent years has contributed to increased administrative discretion in four ways. First, Congress adds to the number of laws requiring interpretive regulation. Second, increased legislative output often produces vague policy statements that later require detailed administrative interpretation. Third, in addition to regulations for meeting the direct purpose of a grant, Congress originates many cross-cutting requirements applicable to other national objectives. The reach of these new regulations reflects increased emphasis on social conditions as opposed to narrow administrative procedures. Fourth, regulations grow because over time Congress and the administration add new restrictions to programs. For example, the New Federalism concept of block grants with fewer strings attached has been weakened by federal bureaucrats who now place increased restrictions on these grants.

The number and the length of federal regulations has grown dramatically. All proposed and final regulations are published in the *Federal Register,* which contained approximately 20,000 pages in 1970; by 1978 it had exceeded 61,000 pages. Although these regulations also govern private institutions, the trend clearly is toward greater regulation of state and local agencies.

The Costs of Regulation

Regulations also may be implemented by memoranda, technical guidance letters, grant application letters, or oral instructions.[2] Often these regulations are interpretive, making policy where laws are vague— frequently requiring wholesale changes in local programs or mandating costly new programs. As a result, local officials repeatedly arrive at conventions and meetings armed with a series of resolutions opposing "intrusive, statutorily unauthorized, excessive, overly restrictive, burdensome and arbitrary" regulations.[3]

In some cases the costs imposed by regulations can impose major burdens on local governments. Consider the Department of Transportation (DOT) rules on access for the handicapped and EPA's regulations to protect municipal drinking water. DOT's draft regulations implementing Section 504 of the Rehabilitation Act of 1973 require that all public transportation be accessible to the handicapped. Opponents of the regulations charge that these mandated improvements are too costly for jurisdictions already squeezed by tax base erosion and taxpayer revolts.

Washington, D.C.'s Metro is the most accessible subway system in America. The elaborate system of DOT-mandated escalators and elevators will cost an estimated $72 million by the time the 100 mile system is complete. Some critics question its cost-effectiveness. When the first 23 miles opened for operation, only 12 wheelchair-bound people commuted by Metro each day. In other areas of transportation, there are additional doubts about the efficacy of the regulations. The transbus—with wide front doors, low steps, ramps, and lifts that provide easy access for wheelchairs—costs 40 to 50 percent more than standard carriers. Cities that have purchased the transbus experience additional problems because the buses frequently have major mechanical problems, boosting maintenance costs.

To the surprise of many local officials, these new and costly regulations were adopted without close review by Congress. DOT's regulations are based on a single sentence in the Rehabilitation Act of 1973, which provides that "no otherwise qualified individual ... shall ... be excluded from participation in ... any program or activity receiving federal financial assistance." It is difficult to determine if it was the intent of Congress to mandate this new spending program since Section 504 was adopted without hearings or significant floor debate.[4] Instead of requiring that entire transportation systems be accessible to the handicapped, city officials would have preferred rules allowing them the freedom to decide if a particular mode of alternative transportation, such as a dial-a-ride service, is more responsive to the needs of the handicapped.

A second controversy illustrating the importance of regulations surrounds EPA's proposed initiative to reduce the level of harmful organic contaminants in drinking water. If adopted, the regulations would set a maximum allowable level of organic chemicals in water systems in cities with populations of more than 75,000, and require the monitoring of water systems in towns with populations of 10,000 to 75,000. The most costly feature of the proposed regulation is the use of granular activated carbon filters to control organic chemicals in water systems serving more than 75,000 people. EPA estimated the cost for implementing these regulations would be from $600 million to $800 million. The Coalition for Safe Drinking Water, a group of private utilities and public agencies opposing the regulations, estimated the costs to be more than double EPA's estimates—$1.87

billion. Many city officials argue that EPA has not adequately documented the health risks of the chemicals. Moreover, they claim the monitoring and treatment standards are beyond the fiscal means of most cities.

These two programs promised to add between $3 billion and $13 billion to the cost of urban government. Given these high stakes, it is not surprising that, as two observers argue, "the guideline process constitutes the cutting edge of administrative power." [5] Although a legalistic approach suggests that regulations flow from a detailed study of a bill's language and history, regulation writing is often more dynamic. It is not always easy to define legislative intent since coalition building frequently unites factions with different and sometimes conflicting goals. The result of this is "laws that are vague, imprecise, and even contradictory on exactly those issues that are the most conceptually troublesome and politically controversial." [6]

In other cases, legislation is vague or requires administrative interpretation because Congress simply fails to understand the complexities of program implementation. For example, when Congress passed the Federal Water Pollution Control Act in 1972 it set goals of zero-discharge into the nation's waterways by 1985. According to John Quarles, a former EPA official, "those who originated the standards and those who approved them had no estimates at all of what the costs might be." [7] In fact, Congress often passes legislation without a clear understanding of the practical consequences or actual costs for state or local governments.

In another instance, the Public Welfare Amendments of 1962 initiated a grant-in-aid program for state social services without defining the services qualifying for a 75 percent federal reimbursement. When facing difficult issues, according to Wilbur Cohen, a former HEW assistant secretary for legislation, the tendency was to say: "Put it in the regulations ... do it later." [8] This imprecision guaranteed that key issues would be reopened every time program leadership changed.

One result of vague legislation is a highly political regulatory process, as different actors enter the process over time. In the case of the 1962 Public Welfare Amendments, a loss of fiscal control changed a $350 million program into a $2.5 billion program because different program managers and presidential appointees changed the guidelines as they went along. The 1962 amendments authorized federal payment at 75 percent of the cost to states for eligible social services, but the law did not define these services. Rather, it merely stated their purpose. It referred to self-support, self-care, strengthening family life, and reducing dependency, as the goals of the services. In 1967 new Social Security Amendments required that childcare and family planning services be provided to people in work-training programs.[9] Thus, federal funds were authorized, but services were not mandated nor were the levels of adequacy defined.

The lack of spending limits and vague definitions later allowed for rapid expansion of the program. The original regulations, prepared by professional social workers in HEW's Bureau of Family Services, maintained strict control over the reimbursement process. A new group of civil servants drafted more flexible regulations in the late 1960s. A third round of guidelines, promulgated later by Nixon appointees, responded to pressure from several Republican governors interested in underwriting state budgets. In this way, the changing goals of guideline writers over a period of ten years converted a small program into a large program that *The Washington Post* called "backdoor revenue sharing." [10] In fiscal 1973 state reimbursement requests for providing social services totalled $4.7 billion. In response to these requests, Congress placed a $2.5 billion ceiling on the program, which remained in place until fiscal 1979. The spending limit was raised to $3.1 billion in fiscal 1980 and to $3.3 billion for fiscal 1985.

Formulation of Regulations

Several layers of the bureaucracy often work on the same regulations. Particularly costly or controversial regulations frequently are reviewed by the Office of Management and Budget, the Council of Economic Advisers, and the White House staff. President Carter's Executive Order 12044 created a Regulatory Analysis Review Group (RARG) composed of his economic advisers, and representatives from OMB and several cabinet-level agencies, who annually review 10 to 20 regulations chosen on the basis of their inflationary impact. To date, RARG has focused on those regulations affecting private industry, not state and local governments.[11] Regulations are reviewed at almost every step down the bureaucratic ladder. Officials at the assistant secretary or subcabinet level review important agency regulations. Middle level executives, the bureau chiefs or office heads, make basic policy determinations, and civil servants implement these decisions.

Regulations are written according to a predetermined routine in many agencies. In 1973, for example, HEW (now the Department of Health and Human Services) created an Office of Program Implementation to develop and monitor health regulations. HEW's four-step system was typical of the process used in many other agencies. First, an internal office developed an issue specification document, called a SPEC, stating the concerns to be addressed by the regulations. Second, a Draft Notice of Proposed Rule Making (Draft NPRM), or rough draft of the regulations, was cleared with other units within HEW. Third, a Notice of Proposed Rulemaking (NPRM) was prepared for and reviewed by the secretary. This notice was then published in the *Federal Register*, with a request for comments from interested groups or individuals. Finally, after public comment, the regulations were revised and published in final form.[12]

As one might guess, the regulatory process can be very lengthy. Often regulations for a program are published separately, as each part is completed. Several years may pass before a complete set of regulations becomes final. For example, EPA issued hazardous waste regulations under the Resource Conservation and Recovery Act (RCRA) of 1976 in seven packages during 1979 and 1980, more than two years after the statutory guideline for promulgating regulations passed. The delays in issuing these regulations prevented many states from developing their own programs to control hazardous industrial chemicals. Delays of this sort in the rulemaking process often can be as frustrating as the final regulatory requirements themselves. Yet extensive comment from, and participation by, state and local governments and public interest groups also contributes to delays in guideline writing. Comments on HUD's eligibility and allocation rules for urban counties, numbering over 200, helped delay promulgation of the Community Development Block Grant rules for more than two years.

During the last several years there has been an increase in the participation of state and local groups in the regulation-writing process. Most public interest groups are not content, however, with their participation in the regulatory process. All too often, they argue, comments are requested only when the regulations are released to the public in draft form. However, some agencies, such as the Economic Development Administration and HUD, seem to do a better job than others of inviting state or local officials to participate in the initial drafting.

Even when the public interest groups do participate, they are not always satisfied with the results. In some cases, groups such as mayors and governors may take opposing stands. In other instances, elected officials find that groups of state and local program specialists carry more clout with regulation writers. Finally, private associations like the U.S. Chamber of Commerce or the National Association of Homebuilders can use their greater resources to support regulations that are objectionable to state and local groups.

Nonetheless, many state and local officials actively participate in the process of writing regulations. Hundreds of comments frequently are received on proposed regulations. After the National Governors' Conference objected that proposed regulations under the Health Maintenance Organization Act of 1973 would erode its role in federal, state, and local health planning, HEW invited the governors to participate in the regulation-writing process. The governors were concerned that the Health Maintenance Organization (HMO) regulations would threaten the states' role in health planning and regulation as well as their control over allocating grants. After complaining to HEW, the National Governors' Conference obtained some concessions on the regulatory language. In fact, HEW provided them with a grant to hold public meetings and to research state positions. So, when it is important to reach a consensus, the regulated groups may be able to make successful claims for access to decisionmakers.[13]

In 1979 the Washington Office of the Council of State Governments worked to prevent the General Services Administration from restricting permanently the use of certain kinds of surplus federal property that was leased to the states. Working with officials in OMB and HEW, the Council of State Governments was able to convince the General Services Administration not to publish the rule.[14]

Thus, administrative regulations do more than rationalize public policy. They also serve as a political scoreboard registering the skill and strength of various actors. According to two observers, regulations and other guidelines:

> formulated by compromise among political and bureaucratic actors may also defeat the distinctive purposes guidelines are expected to serve, fragment control beyond repair, and thereby place unintended obstacles in the way of the public's attempt to hold government officials accountable for the words by which we are governed.[15]

In fact, Congress is increasingly including in its legislation the authorization of the legislative veto, a controversial device that allows it to veto administrative regulations. To date, Congress actually has used the legislative veto only occasionally to block newly promulgated regulations.

ALLOCATING FUNDS

Use of Formulas

Federal bureaucrats annually make thousands of decisions to allocate federal funds. As shown in Table 5-1, during 1978 approximately two-thirds of the 492 categorical or narrow purpose grants were project grants. These are grants that allow agency officials to determine which applications will be funded. Yet in the largest categorical programs a formula is most often used to distribute funds. Although project grants account for two-thirds of the grant programs, they distribute less than one-quarter of all federal transfer payments to

Table 5-1. Number of Categorical Grants, by Type, Fiscal Years 1975, 1978.

	1975		1978	
	Number	*Percent*	*Number*	*Percent*
Formula-based				
allotted formula	96	21.7	106	21.5
Project grants subject to formula distribution	35	7.9	47	9.6
Open-end reimbursement	15	3.4	17	3.5
Total formula-based	146	33.0	170	34.6
Project	296	67.0	322	65.4
Total	442	100.0	492	100.0

SOURCE: U.S. Advisory Commission on Intergovernmental Relations staff tabulations.

state and local governments. There are, as J. Theodore Anagnoson notes, "a large number of project grants, each distributing relatively small amounts of money, and a small number of formula grants, each distributing relatively large amounts of money." [16]

Congress prefers to allocate the big transfer payments directly to subnational governments. When the financial stakes are large, Congress often creates a formula within the law to determine the allocation to eligible governments. The result is to guarantee funds to state and local governments based on economic or demographic factors outlined in the formula. Formula grants also reduce the discretion of federal administrators in the review process.

Project grants, those categorical grants where federal administrators can select which applications to fund, theoretically can be focused on problem areas. Administrators award grants to local or state governments based on information contained in competitive applications. In practice, however, civil servants often act like legislators when they allocate funds. That is, they spread funds across as many congressional districts as possible. According to one Brookings Institution study, "even though project grants are not distributed by legislative formula, federal agencies tend to use their own administratively determined formulas to set aside funds for each state or region in the country." [17]

When Congress chooses not to select a formula, why would administrators restrict their own flexibility by adopting one? Administrators may do this for several reasons. One reason may be that administrators place a premium on building geographically broad support for programs to avoid criticism during congressional oversight or appropriations hearings. To maintain this support, it may be necessary to guarantee a fair share of the resources to each region, state, or congressional district. Administrators also protect themselves from charges of favoritism by designing apparently objective allocation criteria.

Agencies can insulate themselves from political pressure through three related processes. First, a decentralized project selection process allows for regional or area office evaluation. Second, a set of guidelines are written into administrative allocation formulas to spread the funds across many jurisdictions. Third, an ambiguous method for assessing project benefits allows civil servants to ensure that few states or areas are left without a project.[18]

Guidelines that spread the funds around are at the center of the process. There are precise formulas to guarantee that no region or state receives too many or too few awards. Agencies avoid precise definitions of project merit and rely on rules linked to minimums, maximums, and quotas.

For example, the Economic Development Administration (EDA) uses five basic factors to allocate its public works grants. First, national appropriations are allocated to EDA regional offices based on area size and population—guaranteeing that every region receives a portion of the total. Second, legislative limits hold any state's share to no more than 15 percent of the national total. This prevents any one state from consuming a large portion of total appropriations. Third, every state is guaranteed at least one area that is eligible for EDA public works grants. Fourth, EDA discourages projects over $1 million because a few large projects can lock out many smaller ones. Finally, the Economic Development Administration limits the number of projects in any urban area.[19]

Similarly, HUD's distribution of water and sewer funds from 1966 to 1974 provided for broad political coverage rather than targeting. Prior to 1974 when Congress merged the water and sewer grant program with the Community Development Block Grant, allocations to HUD regional and area offices were based on the number of housing units. HUD also imposed a $1.5 million limit on the federal share of any project and developed guidelines to fund only one project annually in any urban area (two in larger metropolitan areas). Steps were taken to guarantee that no congressional district received more than one grant a year. These mechanisms prevented a few cities or areas from consuming the lion's share of the resources, and it redistributed funds from a few large metropolitan areas to large numbers of suburban and rural communities.[20]

In summary, administrative control over subnational governments is not as large as critics of bureaucratic discretion allege: approximately three-quarters of all intergovernmental funds are allocated by legislative formula. Once a formula is established, the allocation criteria are altered only with great difficulty. While the types of grants may vary from president to president, the geographic distribution is very stable over time. Congressional interest in resource distribution protects state and local governments from sudden changes. In 1977, for example, Congress reacted very negatively to President Carter's proposals to improve targeting of federal aid, and "hold harmless" clauses were enacted to protect jurisdictions from immediate cutbacks. When allocations are based on political factors, it later becomes very difficult to impose sanctions or terminate funds for poor performance.

Political Constraints

Despite forces encouraging federal aid administrators to distribute grant funds broadly, monies cannot be distributed evenly. Two factors— political clout and grantsmanship skills—account for significant variations in receipt of project grants across individual jurisdictions in a region or state. If a governor or a mayor is a member of the president's political party, the chances of influencing allocations may be enhanced. In 1971, the Republican governor of Illinois, Richard Ogilvie, pressured President Nixon's appointees in HEW and on the White House staff to loosen the definition of reimbursable social services. This alteration increased the flow of public assistance funds to Illinois and helped the governor to balance his election year budget. The spending explosion for social services discussed earlier in this chapter flows, in part, from an attempt to play politics with social services. Martha Derthick concludes that "federal policy was being shaped to meet the needs of the governor of Illinois." [21]

Another asset in the competition for grants can be the political connections of the area's congressional representative. Project grants act as grease when administrators apply them to important joints in the legislative machinery. In July 1978, HUD Secretary Patricia Harris announced the creation of 89 urban development action grants. Approximately 73 percent of the $262 million in awards went to cities represented by members of the House or Senate committees overseeing HUD activities. Asked about this relationship, Secretary Harris denied favoritism. "I'm asking you to believe," said Harris, "that those cities have great need and that they have recognized this need by electing outstanding leaders of the House and Senate." [22]

If political connections can work in favor of a jurisdiction's ability to obtain federal grants, they can also work against it. In November

1979, after Mayor Jane Byrne of Chicago endorsed Senator Ted Kennedy for president, Neil Goldschmidt, President Carter's secretary of Transportation, declared that he had "lost confidence" in Mayor Byrne and would not look favorably on her city's application for discretionary funds. This announcement caused quite a commotion; Goldschmidt, along with several other cabinet members, was charged in a civil suit for using federal offices and public funds to promote the president's bid for reelection. Although Secretary Goldschmidt later backtracked a bit, claiming that his "personal problem" with Byrne would not work against the people of Chicago, political advisors to the president indicated that Carter was happy to see his cabinet playing political hardball in an election year.[23]

Grantsmanship

The sophistication of local officials also can explain the allocation of some federal dollars. Towns, rural counties, and small cities that cannot afford their own Washington lobbyist or grants coordinator may find this a distinct disadvantage when competing for federal funds. In larger jurisdictions, increases in staff grantsmanship skills clearly bring visible results. However, in rural areas, one person—the mayor, the city manager, or a consultant—can make a big difference. Ingenuity at filling out applications or at identifying funding sources allows some small towns to "strike it rich." Mayor John Henry Moss of Kings Mountain, North Carolina, attracted over $16 million to his small town in ten years, obtaining support for a community center, a large water project, a waste-water treatment plan, and $4.5 million for urban renewal. Mayor Moss's "Midas touch" can be traced to his reading habits, including ten hours weekly devoted to the *Catalog of Federal Assistance.* After advisory committees complete the legwork, Mayor Moss personally fills out the applications and follows through with the federal bureaucracy, producing a success story matched in very few towns.[24]

Similar successes can result from aggressive grantsmanship by local administrators. Blades, Delaware, a poor town of 650 people, received approximately $2.3 million in federal grants in 1977. That amounts to $3,700 per person. The federal grants that Blades received included $930,000 from the Economic Development Administration for a water system, $245,000 from HUD for housing rehabilitation and planning, and $1.15 million from EPA for a sewer system. Henry Flood, a young community development specialist, was responsible for this abundance of funds. As an administrative assistant to the district's state senator, Flood began uncovering detailed income data on Blades that the Census Bureau had lumped together with data from a larger, more affluent, neighboring community. After Flood demonstrated that the average income in Blades was $3,000 less than in its neighbor, eligibility for several new grants was established. Once the town's needs were documented, Flood applied his knowledge of the grants process to marshall support for community development projects.[25]

In other areas, consultants are the key to obtaining federal dollars. In 1977 HUD allocated its entire $500,000 Pennsylvania allocation for a small city community development award to one town, Whitehall Township, an affluent suburb of Allentown with a population of 25,000. The town's need, as measured by median income, was lower than all but one other applicant. Yet Whitehall's consultant, Steven Weinberg, discovered how to exploit the HUD decisionmaking process.

The Department of Housing and Urban Development relies on written applications from small communities and not on field inspections. Since the law identifies low income people, not low income communities, as the target beneficiaries, a rich community intending to target funds on "poverty pockets" can apply for funds. Weinberg documented that one poor section of town with 55 percent "low income" residents, needed help. HUD's allocation system also awarded points to towns receiving outside funding. A modest $2,000 grant from Pennsylvania's Department of Community Affairs, obtained by Weinberg, yielded the maximum score in this rating category. Weinberg's thorough knowledge of HUD's rating system, familiarity with census data, and the ability to obtain state funding enabled Whitehall to win the entire $500,000 allocation.[26]

PROBLEMS OF FEDERAL ORGANIZATION FOR GRANT DELIVERY

Administrative problems plague the federal government's dealings with states and localities. The regulations accompanying federal grants also impose considerable financial costs and project delays on state and local governments. According to many officials, there are too many programs run by too many federal agencies. Others see the intergovernmental grants system as overly centralized because area and regional federal officials lack the authority to respond directly to local problems. Additionally, efforts to coordinate federal programs are ineffective because narrow program specific issues override concerns for the entire grant-in-aid process.

Duplication of Effort

Categorical programs, enacted to benefit comparatively few groups and serving a narrow purpose, continue to grow. The largest increases

Table 5-2. Categorical Grant Programs, by Budget Subfunction[a] and Grant Type: Fiscal Years 1975 and 1978.

Budget Subfunction	FY 1975	FY 1978	Change 1975-78
Department of Defense—Military	5	5	—
General Science and Basic Research	1	1	—
Energy	—	6	+ 6
Water Resources	7	7	—
Conservation and Land Management	12	13	+ 1
Recreational Resources	8	10	+ 2
Pollution Control and Abatement	23	35	+12
Other Natural Resources	5	4	− 1
Agricultural Research and Services	8	9	+ 1
Mortgage Credit and Thrift Insurance	2		—
Other Advancement and Regulation of Commerce	4	2	− 2
Ground Transportation	32	36	+ 4
Water Transportation	4	2	− 2
Mass Transportation	5	8	+ 3
Air Transportation	3	3	—
Other Transportation	1	1	—
Community Development	15	5	−10
Area and Regional Development	27	36	+ 9
Disaster Relief and Insurance	9	9	—
Elementary, Secondary, and Vocational Education	78	70	− 8
Higher Education	9	10	+ 1
Research and General Education Aids	13	21	+ 8
Training and Employment	19	23	+ 4
Other Labor Services	1	1	—
Social Services	36	47	+11
Health	71	78	+ 7
Public Assistance and Other Income Supplements	22	27	+ 5
Hospital and Medical Care for Veterans	6	5	− 1
Criminal Justice Assistance	13	13	—
General Property and Records Management	1	1	—
Other General Government	2	2	—
Totals	442	490	+50

[a] Except for health programs.
SOURCE: Advisory Commission on Intergovernmental Relations, *A Catalog of Federal Grant-In-Aid Programs to State and Local Governments: Grants Funded FY 1978.* (Washington, D.C.: U.S. Government Printing Office, 1979), p. 2.

are in the areas of pollution control, economic development, health, and energy. According to the ACIR's 1978 scorecard on federal grants as shown in Table 5-2, 78 categorical grants existed for health along with 70 for education. Grants for social services numbered 47, while 36 existed for both regional development and ground transportation. Often countless narrow programs exist within a single department. In 1978 the undisputed leader was HEW, which administered 220 grant programs before its reorganization. HEW was followed by the departments of Transportation and Agriculture with 50 and 42 respectively, and by EPA with 35.[27]

The complexity of the system, as well as the narrow focus of many programs, presents overwhelming barriers to coordination by the nation's cities, counties, and states. Programs often are too restrictive or too narrowly defined when they reach the state or local level. Grantees then waste valuable time trying to discern relatively small differences in emphasis between programs and among agencies. Elmer Staats, comptroller general of the United States, remarking on a General Accounting Office study, told Congress: "Many of the problems associated with our domestic assistance efforts are directly attributable to the large number of programs and the proliferation of responsibility among different departments and agencies."[28]

Regulations governing categorical programs often are restrictive, conflicting, and confusing. The number of grants alone vastly understates the complexity of grants management. Numerous cross-cutting regulatory requirements raise the number of required federal clearances necessary for implementation. Even in general revenue sharing, a program that is theoretically free of strings, 15 different agencies play roles by collecting data and monitoring compliance with administrative, nondiscrimination, and other regulations.[29] Additionally, regulations routinely stand as obstacles to joint funding, budgetary transfers, and other measures to help local officials assemble an intergovernmental jigsaw puzzle. Even top level federal executives cannot master the maze of narrow programs. Former HEW Secretary Elliot Richardson once remarked, "the federal program has become so complex that it is unmanageable. Interdependencies among programs are ignored because they cannot be understood, leaving rational choice difficult, if not impossible."[30]

Centralization and Decentralization

Another barrier to responsiveness stems from the high degree of centralization in program administration. Although almost every major domestic agency maintains regional or area offices, in some agencies these officials often lack final grant disbursement authority.

Grants are delayed as officials in Washington review applications that already have been reviewed by regional officials. Local officials often feel frustrated when they know that the federal field representatives with whom they work do not make the final decisions. In some agencies, such as HUD and EPA, there is a good deal of decentralization, but in others, such as HEW, far less discretion rests with field officials. Some bureaucrats argue that there are benefits to be gained from greater decentralization. According to one HUD regional official, "Regional concerns would be swallowed up if we were in Washington under the shadow of the whole federal government." "Every state problem we deal with has a unique character," maintains an EPA regional official, "it's our job to know them better than Washington ever could." [31] However, the balance clearly remains tilted toward Washington—regional offices are able to approve project grant applications or plan amendments for formula grants in only 40 percent of the categorical programs.[32]

Despite some recent movement toward decentralization, the discretion of regional actors still varies greatly among departments and across programs in individual agencies. Often statutory requirements bind their hands, but in other programs national bureaucrats refuse to surrender authority to field subordinates. Decentralization raises problems of national consistency and also requires a rare commitment on the part of top management to make it effective. William Ruckelshaus, EPA's first administrator, is one example of an executive who was willing to delegate major responsibilities to regional offices. He believed that the capacity to run a wide range of programs had to accompany delegated responsibility and decided that "each regional organization should mirror the full EPA structure, with staff capabilities in every program area." As a result, EPA is more decentralized than many other agencies in the federal government. According to one former EPA official, "In view of the immense complexity of EPA's programs, the agency's progress would have been tightly restricted if it had not built a strong regional structure right from the start." [33]

Attempts to Improve Coordination

Federal Regional Councils. To remedy problems spawned by proliferating grant programs, numerous middle range efforts to improve coordination have been attempted during the last decade. On balance, they have achieved only limited results. In 1969, for example, President Nixon created ten Federal Regional Councils (FRCs) to serve each of the newly organized standard federal administrative regions shown in Figure 5-1. President Nixon charged the FRCs, composed of the principal regional officials of 11 domestic agencies, with resolving

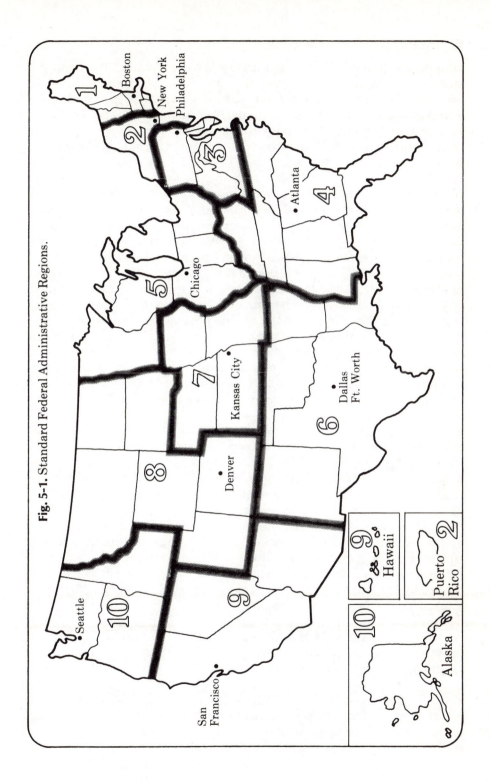

Fig. 5-1. Standard Federal Administrative Regions.

interagency disputes in the field, coordinating programs, and handling intergovernmental relations. According to President Nixon, "Such councils can make it possible for the federal government to speak consistently with a single voice in its dealings with states and localities, with private organizations and with the public." [34]

Although each FRC is chaired by a regional official designated by the president, they have never been strongly supported by the president or Congress. President Nixon failed to give FRC heads strong administrative powers; as a result of this limited authority, they serve only as political spokespersons for the current administration. Despite some notable successes, such as the coordination of grants to Pennsylvania to cope with the impact of the Three Mile Island nuclear incident, the overall record is not impressive.

During the Nixon and Ford administrations, the FRCs reported to the Office of Management and Budget and to the Undersecretaries Group, a high-level interdepartmental group. In the Carter administration, the FRCs reported to an Inter-Agency Coordinating Committee (IACC) chaired by Jack Watson, the assistant to the president for intergovernmental affairs. Although the IACC expanded FRC membership and upgraded their powers somewhat, official Washington remains largely indifferent to their operations. According to one observer, Wes Uhlman, former mayor of Seattle, "The councils were delivered to us in a great throes of a public relations effort by President Nixon. I am not sure he really believed in them. Certainly, the bureaucrats didn't, as they did their best to undermine them. But the concept is a good one. That is why they have survived so far." [35]

The lack of official support was reflected in the failure of presidents Nixon, Ford, and Carter to give FRC heads the authority and independent staff to perform their assignments. As a result, each council lacks the clout to deal with regional problems. This is compounded by the fact that some FRC member agencies—Agriculture, Commerce, Health and Human Services, Interior, and Transportation—are fragmented at the regional level. Regional effectiveness is further handicapped by the fact that not all federal agencies have regional boundaries conforming to the standard designations.

Joint Funding and Simplification Act. Other middle range approaches to grants reform encourage state and local governments to set grant priorities while charging federal civil servants with responding to local plans. For example, in 1974 Congress enacted the Joint Funding and Simplification Act, designed to allow state and local governments to use federal assistance more effectively by drawing on resources from more than one federal program. Under this act subnational governments can simultaneously apply for two or more grants and then administer them under one common set of grant conditions and administrative requirements. Three years after enactment, an OMB study found that actual implementation of the act was "virtually negligible." By 1979, only approximately 30 national joint-funded projects existed.[36] According to OMB, federal agencies have not made a commitment to implementation, and there is widespread ignorance of the process at both the national and regional levels. The implementation of joint funding also is restrained by the voluntary nature of the process for federal agencies.

Circular A-95. A more widespread reform is OMB's Circular A-95, implementing the Intergovernmental Cooperation Act of 1968. Circular A-95 established a Project Notification and Review System for state and local agencies to review and evaluate grant applications from area governments. This reform, sparked by pleas from elected officials and their generalist staffs, creates clearinghouses, usually state or regional planning agencies, where the review of grant applications can take place. One problem is that the large volume of applications handled by clearinghouse agencies limits the analysis and comments that are then passed along to federal agencies. Also contributing to the problem is the large number of A-95 notifications that must be processed in a relatively short time.

One result of A-95 is that it reduces the frequency with which program managers bypass elected officials in their search for federal aid. A-95 helps to establish systematic, regular, regional assessment of federal grant activities. It does not necessarily improve coordination among the federal agencies that are asked to consider clearinghouse comments during the review process. Federal managers, as well as many state and local officials, generally view A-95 certification as another hurdle to be jumped before funds can be obligated.

In summary, A-95 serves as a valuable tool for the exchange of information among levels of government. However, the circular's thrust is to coordinate state and local responses to federal programs rather than to forge coordinative links between federal agencies. The ACIR notes, "A-95, as presently conceived, is an alternative to Federal interagency coordination rather than a spur to it." [37]

None of these efforts to coordinate domestic assistance programs—the FRCs, joint funding, A-95 review—yields anything beyond limited or case-by-case results. Program managers, who are accountable to congressional subcommittees and dependent upon national interest groups for support, have few incentives to streamline their requirements and coordinate programs. Top agency managers focus on their individual program, not on that program's effect on the federal system. Presidential staff members and OMB personnel recognize the problem, but lack the incentive or commitment to improve grants management—more dramatic issues and crises drive grants reform off their agendas. The result is that special interests stoutly defend each program's requirements, and no one aggressively monitors the existing reforms to make them work. In short, few actors at the federal level have the time and interest to attempt to sort out a confusing aggregation of grants and regulations.

FEDERAL OVERSIGHT AND EVALUATION

Does the federal government enforce grant-in-aid regulations? Do federal programs regulate subnational governments or do they serve subnational governments? Actually, federal grants implementation accomplishes a bit of each goal. Under many circumstances, however, federal agencies deploy resources and monitor their use in order to develop a constituency relationship; as a result grantees are in a position to use federal programs to serve local goals. State and local officials can exercise influence over federal actors at this phase of the implementation process.

The Politics of Oversight

At the core of federal grants management is the fact that HUD, EPA, DOT, and other agencies operate within a federal system. Every cabinet secretary or agency administrator is responsible to Congress—which represents local interests. As legislators expand their casework activities and service orientation, direct relationships are forged between legislative staff and federal central office and field personnel. Congress often makes it difficult for administrators to set performance standards because the drive to enact legislation means expanding the list of goals and objectives. Often it is not clear whether grants programs are designed to impose federal objectives or underwrite state programs. As a result, legislation represents compromises between advocates and opponents of federal action. According to Phillip Monypenny:

> The opponents of a given federal action may lose out because they are not quite as powerful in Congress or in the federal executive as they are in the state legislative or in the governor's office. They are never without some influence in Congress, if only through their own state Congressional representative.[38]

This directly restricts administrators attempting to hold states and localities accountable for performance.

One result of the above condition is that subnational officials frequently view the purpose of federal grants as the improvement of existing programs. For example, President Johnson pushed a National

Teacher Corps as part of the Higher Education Act of 1965. The primary goal of the Teacher Corps was to send specially trained, innovative teams of young, talented teachers into the schools to educate the poor. Although it was initially seen as a way to reform local education practices, Congress handed over administrative control to the local school districts. As a result, the very institutions that were the target of the reform gained control over the program.

The necessity of building support in Congress for the Teacher Corps also conflicted with the need for clear objectives and standards. According to one Teacher Corps staff member, "We used every argument we could when we were selling the Teacher Corps idea because we had to in order to win support. . . . so we sold it as a manpower program to some people, and just about everything else that was related, and along the way we certainly were guilty of overpromising." Despite Johnson's emphasis on innovation, predictable results followed. According to Thomas E. Cronin, "local school principals and local schools of education believed that the funds were available for them to do a better job of what they were already doing." [39]

Monitoring Performance

Because legislative goals tend to be stated in broad terms, administrators find it conceptually and politically troublesome to construct substantive measures of state and local performance in grant-in-aid programs. However, as the mountains of audits, forms, and reports will attest, this doesn't prevent administrators from monitoring grant recipients. These reports tend to stress administrative conditions, efficiency, and sound management practices rather than improvement in social conditions and, as Martha Derthick has pointed out, the emphasis on administrative factors develops because such criteria avoid controversial value choices. [40] This allows programs to continue without undermining fragile legislative coalitions.

Monitoring and evaluation are usually undertaken by those implementing the program, and the agency often lacks the resources to monitor grant programs. As a case in point, in 1979 the Treasury Department candidly acknowledged that it could not adequately enforce all the federal requirements attached to general revenue sharing. It simply lacked the auditors necessary to check on the 770 complaints about program-related civil rights violations by state and local governments. [41] Even if the federal officials have the resources to monitor grant programs adequately, they may have few incentives to monitor state and local spending aggressively. In many cases the same officials are charged with developing, implementing, and monitoring grant programs. This merging of roles at times leads to a reluctance to take steps that might uncover poor performance.

The various oversight mechanisms give federal policymakers an incomplete understanding of complex intergovernmental transactions. According to Robert Graham, Washington's state auditor, "follow-up assessments have been fragmented and noncomprehensive, providing inadequate information for congressional and legislative groups to base decisions for expansion, continuance or termination." [42] One result is that Washington lacks information on entire programs—the state and local portions as well as the federally funded portions. Furthermore, imperfect program integration compounds the problems of federal oversight and this leads to uneven compliance with federal regulations.

As important as grant auditing is, a General Accounting Office (GAO) study found that federal agency approaches to grant auditing are not coordinated. GAO also concluded that agencies audit only their own grants and pay little attention to how a jurisdiction's grant management practices affect other federal grants. "Under this narrow approach," according to GAO, "the auditors are unlikely to detect improper charges or transfers of funds and equipment to grants." Moreover, some programs are audited repeatedly with minimal results while many programs go unaudited.[43]

An analysis of the Elementary and Secondary Education Act of 1965 by Jerome Murphy of Harvard University provided one explanation of this monitoring problem. He concluded that individual federal agencies may have little inclination to monitor state or local disbursements of federal grants. Despite federal rhetoric regarding the need for evaluation, program evaluation had a low priority at the U.S. Office of Education. Several factors explained the lack of interest in oversight and evaluation, according to Murphy:

> One was the desire not to upset the federal-state balance. Another was recognition that little expertise existed at the state and local levels to evaluate a broad-scale reform program. A third was fear of disclosing failure; no administrator is anxious to show that his program is not working well. Aside from these impediments to effective evaluation, the diverse purposes of Title I left unclear just how one would determine whether Title I was "working." [44]

Even when HEW grant administrators knew of violations of grant requirements, they failed to administer the law aggressively or follow up on the audits. Federal officials consciously tried to limit conflict between levels of government because conflict might indicate problems with the program. Moreover, many Office of Education staff members did not agree with the stated goals of the law and deliberately attempted to undermine the legislation.

One might argue that these conditions apply only to education, but they also appear in other federal agencies. There are many examples of limited implementation and oversight by federal agencies.

For example, in the early 1970s HEW designed regulations to establish parameters of consent for elective sterilization for competent persons over the age of 21. As of March 1975, however, "the sterilization guidelines are being widely ignored, if not deliberately evaded." One study determined that only 2 of the 51 teaching hospitals sampled were in compliance with the federal sterilization regulations.[45] Yet no federal funds were withdrawn from these hospitals. Similarly, civil rights and affirmative action compliance is weak—the lack of personnel may explain a portion of the noncompliance, but the complexities of the regulations and the philosophical positions of the administrators should also be considered.

Clearly, strict federal monitoring is not automatic; it results from political and organizational decisions. The strength of federal leadership may vary from program to program or within a single program over the years. One case in point is the social service program examined earlier in this chapter. As you will recall, the reimbursable social service program expanded because of a vague law, the lack of a spending ceiling, and the changing orientations of the civil servants and political appointees who directed the program. In fact, Martha Derthick concludes, "spending got out of control because the sponsoring bureau, which was professionally specialized in giving social services, lost jurisdiction and no effective organization took its place." [46]

Given this condition, and compliance patterns by state agencies, a clear picture of the weaknesses in intergovernmental linkages emerges. Even in a visible social policy area like abortion, federal influence is limited. The Supreme Court, in its 1973 decision, *Roe* v. *Wade,* struck down restrictive state abortion laws; in 1977 the Court decided that states need not use public funds to provide abortions to the poor. Nonetheless, Planned Parenthood estimated that prior to the Court's 1977 decision, 80 percent of the nation's public hospitals excluded abortion services—failing to comply with HEW Medicaid regulations. Furthermore, in ten states no abortions at all were performed during 1974.[47]

Federal Enforcement

Given the tendency of federal agencies to form constituency links with grant recipients, it is not surprising that federal enforcement of regulations is often weak. Ambiguous goals and staff constraints also work against tough enforcement. Federal agencies generally turn to informal bargaining as a way of resolving disputes. The ultimate sanction is the threat to withhold funds—which could be an effective weapon to encourage compliance. In practice, though, funds are rarely withheld—to do so would stop public services and further harm the intended beneficiaries.

In some programs, federal agencies forego the chance to sanction grant recipients. Federal administrators rarely withhold funds or suspend payments as a way to enforce statutory requirements. One 1977 survey shows that only 26 percent of federal grant administrators had withheld or suspended payments to any grantee in the previous five years. According to the ACIR's assistant director, David Walker, "there has been a decline in the practice over the past 11 years, despite the increase in the number and dollar flow of aid programs." [48]

Indeed, the longer programs go without imposing sanctions, the harder it becomes to make threats credible and to reverse longstanding practices. In many agencies the overriding priority simply is disbursing the grant money to grantees as quickly as possible. In Chicago, for example, HUD financed a public housing program operated in a racially discriminatory way throughout the 1960s. HUD's failure to enforce its own regulations can be linked to a reluctance to offend Chicago's Mayor Daley because of his political power in Congress and alliance with several Democratic presidents. In short, administrative attitudes can be more important than the regulations, as building constituency support takes priority over actual administrative practices.[49]

Short of withholding funds, federal agencies can negotiate for compliance with grant regulations. Administrators can also impose costs on grantees by delaying awards or requiring additional paperwork. Through the grants bargaining process, however, federal administrators are more likely to influence administrative operations than public policy. Helen Ingram maintains that this is true because, "As a result of grant bargaining, federal administrative agencies can facilitate change in a willing state. But in the absence of state commitment, the federal agency cannot compel policy change." [50] In short, federal agencies rarely purchase support; grants merely create opportunities for negotiation.

CONCLUSIONS

Federal agencies use grants-in-aid to influence the conduct of state and local governments. Yet this influence is not as strong as often assumed. Federal control is imperfect because the drive to build legislative coalitions creates a conflict among program goals. Additionally, political incentives encourage program managers to distribute benefits broadly, rather than to target grants for excellent programs or needy areas. Other pressures such as constituency building and funds disbursement encourage accommodation to local interests. Although federal regulations and administrative fragmentation impose substantial costs on grantees, it is clear that state and local governments, by mobilizing political support, possess opportunities to influence federal programs and thus to become part of the regulatory process that surrounds the intergovernmental grants process.

The implementation of grants-in-aid programs by federal administrators takes place within an environment of administrative fragmentation. Rather than strict federal control, the process is best characterized by negotiation between the various interests involved. This tends to diffuse authority and control over the system to a very high degree. At this stage in the grants process the role of elected officials becomes more remote as the results of federal grants depend less upon legislative intent than on the complex interactions between administrators in the *regulated* and *regulatory* agencies.

NOTES

1. Several good analyses of this process have appeared recently. See Jeffrey L. Pressman and Aaron B. Wildavsky, *Implementation* (Berkeley, Calif.: University of California Press, 1973); and Eugene Bardach, *The Implementation Game* (Cambridge, Mass.: MIT Press, 1977).
2. Francine Rabinowitz, Jeffrey Pressman and Martin Rein, "Guidelines: A Plethora of Forms, Authors, and Functions," *Policy Sciences* 7 (December 1976): 411.
3. Bill Davis, "Regulations, Costs, Subjects of Policy Debate," *City Weekly* (November 13, 1978), p. 1.
4. Timothy B. Clark, "Access for the Handicapped—A Test for Carter's War on Inflation," *National Journal* 10 (October 21, 1978): 1672-1675.
5. Lawrence D. Brown and Bernard Freiden, "Guidelines and Goals in the Models Cities Program," *Policy Sciences* 7 (December 1976): 466.
6. Ibid., p. 457.
7. John Quarles, *Cleaning Up America: An Insider's View of the Environmental Protection Agency* (Boston: Houghton Mifflin Co., 1976), p. 163.
8. Martha Derthick, *Uncontrollable Spending For Social Service Grants* (Washington, D.C.: Brookings Institution, 1975), p. 9.
9. Marian Lief Palley and Howard A. Palley, *Urban America and Public Policies* (Lexington, Mass.: D. C. Heath & Co., 1977), pp. 121-122.
10. Derthick, *Uncontrollable Spending*, p. 4.
11. Susan J. Tolchin, "Presidential Power and the Politics of RARG," *Regulation* 3 (July/August 1979): 44-49.
12. Drew Altman and Harvey Sapolsky, "Writing Regulations for Health," *Policy Sciences* 7 (December 1976): 419.
13. Ibid., p. 429.
14. Jack McRay, Director Washington Office, The Council of State Governments, May 22, 1980, Washington, D.C.
15. Brown and Frieden, "Guidelines and Goals," p. 488.
16. J. Theodore Anagnoson, "Targeting Federal Grants: An Impossible Dream?" (Paper presented at the Annual Meeting of the American Society for Public Administration, Phoenix, Arizona, 1978), p. 6.
17. Edward R. Fried, Alice M. Rivlin, Charles L. Schultze, and Nancy H. Teeters, *Setting National Priorities: The 1974 Budget* (Washington, D.C.: Brookings Institution, 1973), p. 181.

18. J. Theodore Anagnoson, "Selecting Federal Projects: A Bureaucratic Perspective" (Paper presented at the Annual Meeting of the Midwest Political Science Association, Chicago, Illinois, 1978), p. 7.
19. Ibid., pp. 7-15.
20. Ibid., pp. 15-18.
21. Derthick, *Uncontrollable Spending,* p. 69.
22. Pat Ordovensky, "Grease," *Wilmington* (Del.) *Sunday News-Journal,* July 16, 1978.
23. David E. Rosenbaum, "Goldschmidt: A New Hand for 'Political Arms' " *New York Times,* December 30, 1979, p. 4E.
24. "Midas Touch," *Newsweek* (November 10, 1975), p. 13.
25. Nancy Kesler, "Blades learns Santa Claus lives in Washington," *Wilmington* (Del.) *Sunday News-Journal,* Dec. 11, 1977.
26. Wayne E. Griene, "How a Town Won a Half-Million Pot from HUD Though Poorer Communities Held Strong Hands," *Wall Street Journal,* August 25, 1977, p. 32.
27. Advisory Commission on Intergovernmental Relations, *A Catalog of Federal Grant-in-Aid Programs to State and Local Governments: Grants Funded FY 1978* (Washington, D.C.: U.S. Government Printing Office, 1979).
28. U.S., Senate, Committee on Government Operations, *Hearings: Government Economy and Spending Reform Act* (Washington, D.C.: U.S. Government Printing Office, 1976), p. 157.
29. Richard P. Nathan, Allen D. Maxwell, Susannah E. Calkins, and associates, *Monitoring Revenue Sharing* (Washington, D.C.: Brookings Institution, 1975), pp. 20-23.
30. John K. Inglehart, William Lilly III, and Timothy B. Clarke, "New Federalism Report/HEW Department Advances Sweeping Proposals to Overhaul Its Programs," *National Journal* 5 (January 6, 1973): 3.
31. Bob Levey, "Federal Philadelphia," *Washington Post,* May 10, 1979.
32. U.S. Advisory Commission on Intergovernmental Relations, *Improving Federal Grants Management* (Washington, D.C.: U.S. Government Printing Office, 1977), p. 189.
33. Quarles, *Cleaning Up America,* p. 34.
34. Rochelle L. Stanfield, "Federal Regional Councils—Can Carter Make Them Work?" *National Journal* 9 (June 18, 1977): 950.
35. Ibid., pp. 949-950.
36. U.S., Office of Management and Budget, "Joint Funding Assessment," (Washington, D.C.: Office of Management and Budget, 1977).
37. ACIR, *Improving Federal Grants Management,* p. 283.
38. Phillip Monypenny, "Federal Grants-in-Aid to State Governments: A Political Analysis," *National Tax Journal* 13 (March 1960): 16.
39. Thomas E. Cronin, "Small Program, Big Troubles: Policy-Making for a Small 'Great Society' Program," p. 24.
40. Martha Derthick, *The Influence of Federal Grants* (Cambridge, Mass.: Harvard University Press, 1970), pp. 197-198.
41. John Herbers, "End to Federal Revenue-Sharing Expected in the Forthcoming Budget," *New York Times,* July 9, 1979, p. 16.
42. Robert V. Graham, "Toward a More Effective Audit of Grant-In-Aid Programs," *State Government* 46 (Spring 1973): 119.
43. U.S., General Accounting Office, *Grant Auditing: A Maze of Inconsistency, Gaps, and Duplication that Needs Overhauling* (Washington, D.C.: U.S. Government Printing Office, 1979).

44. Jerome T. Murphy, "The Education Bureaucracies Implement Novel Policy: The Politics of Title I of ESEA, 1965-1972," in *Policy and Politics in America,* ed. Allan P. Sindler (Boston: Little, Brown & Co., 1973), p. 174.
45. Eleanor Krauss, *Hospital Survey on Sterilization Policy* (New York: American Civil Liberties Union, 1975).
46. Derthick, *Uncontrollable Spending,* p. 113.
47. E. Sullivan, C. Tietze, J. Dryfoos, "Legal Abortions in the United States," *Family Planning Perspectives* 9 (May-June 1977): 121.
48. David B. Walker, "Federal Aid Administrators and the Federal System," *Intergovernmental Perspective* 3 (Fall 1977): 14.
49. Frederick Aaron Lazin, "The Failure of Federal Enforcement of Civil Rights Regulations in Public Housing, 1963-71: The Co-optation of a Federal Agency by its Local Constituency," *Policy Sciences* 4 (1973): 263-273.
50. Helen Ingram, "Policy Implementation Through Bargaining: The Case of Federal Grants-in-Aid," *Public Policy* 25 (Fall 1977): 521.

6

The Effect of Grants on State and Local Governments

The increased number of federal grants to state and local governments has helped to expand the role and power of those jurisdictions supported by federal aid. Federal aid has both centralizing and decentralizing tendencies. Increasingly, subnational governments draw upon the national treasury to underwrite the cost of basic, essential services. During program implementation it is not clear where the authority rests. The proliferation of grants, rules, regulations, and funding uncertainties appears to tie the hands of state and local officials, but federal officials are not necessarily in control.

The political effects of federal grants are not simply to shift control from one level of government to another level of government. The very factors that appear to be centralizing influences—grants proliferation, massive funding, and red tape—encourage major redistributions of political power within each unit of government. Influence becomes the property of the bureaucrats who master the complexity of federal grant regulations. In other words, the regulated groups are able to maintain considerable clout in a process ostensibly designed by the regulators to contain their influence. As a result, elected state and local officials find themselves doubly dependent on federal aid and on the skills and knowledge of those administrators. State and local bureaucrats, in turn, often can circumvent federal controls. The very scale of the intergovernmental grants system overly taxes federal administrative skills and creates opportunities for state and local governments to substitute their own program priorities for those of their patrons.

To understand more completely the relationships between the federal government (the regulators) and state and local governments (the regulated), the effects of grants now will be examined. First, there will be a short discussion of the dependence of subnational governments on federal aid. Next, some of the problems and solutions associated with the categorical grants mechanism will be considered. Then block grants and general revenue sharing will be examined. Finally, the source of state and local agency independence and their ability to manipulate federal funds will be examined.

DEPENDENCE ON FEDERAL AID

Local governments are increasingly turning to Washington to finance public buildings, roads, transit facilities, social services, and salaries. In many jurisdictions a cutback in federal aid or even a slowdown in the growth rate of assistance can require drastic program cutbacks or major tax hikes. Large cities have become the most dependent on federal aid during recent years. The urban lobbies formed in the 1960s, along with the poor economic conditions in the mid-1970s, created new support in Congress for local reliance on federal funds.

In 1978 the ACIR concluded that "direct federal aid as a percent of municipal own-source revenue has virtually doubled every five years over the last two decades." [1] Federal aid seems to be necessary if the nation is to attack urban problems. Many hard-pressed units of government are greatly dependent on federal assistance. It is, however, becoming increasingly difficult to sustain political support for increased aid to state and local governments. As early as 1978 the Carter administration notified state and local governments that the heyday of federal assistance had passed. Indeed, total grant outlays grew at substantially less than the rate of inflation during 1979 and 1980. Over the long term, perhaps the only alternative to drastic cuts in services are reforms to make cities and other local governments more self-supporting.

Many cities lack the resources to finance important programs such as housing, mass transit, and water pollution abatement. Milwaukee's mayor, Henry Maier, told a group of mayors in 1978 that "We hear a lot these days about the amount of money going to state and local governments. I think that every mayor here at budget time asks himself this question: 'If we're so rich, how come we didn't get the money to replace the falling-down bridge, or replace all the streets and sewers that are wearing out, or take care of the needs of old, deteriorating public buildings?' " [2]

How long can the federal government continue to increase allocations to the cities? The consequences for local government would be severe if federal aid began to decline. The dependence of subnational governments on federal aid is compounded by complex delivery systems that often bypass elected officials, limiting accountability to the public. Steven Steib and Lynn Rittenhouse, two economists who studied the effects of the grant system on the city of Tulsa, Oklahoma, concluded that, "the existence of easily circumvented state law, topped by the temptation of Federal largesse, has led the city to build a nearly incomprehensible system of public trusts which are, except in name, city departments." [3]

One problem with federal aid is that fiscal pressures tempt many hard-pressed cities to use temporary aid as a permanent crutch. Rather than stimulating new programs or short term activities, many grants underwrite basic and essential services. Today large amounts of federal assistance, especially in broad block or formula grant areas, substitute for local funds. One example of the growing dependence on federal aid and the consequences of cutbacks can be seen in the death of the countercyclical aid program in 1978. In 1976 Congress reacted to a recession by enacting a $3 billion package of countercyclical assistance to state and local governments with very few strings attached. Antirecession funds went to the states and cities with unemployment rates above 4.5 percent when the national rate topped 6 percent. In late 1978 this countercyclical aid died when Congress adjourned without extending the program. Disagreements over targeting aid to the neediest areas, as well as doubts about extending the program after the economy recovered, blocked the necessary legislative action.

The countercyclical program encouraged use of the grants to maintain basic services during a time of fiscal distress. City after city began to treat countercyclical aid as a permanent form of revenue sharing. The death of countercyclical aid, along with cuts and new restrictions on the Comprehensive Employment and Training Act (CETA), came as a crushing blow to many cities. Pittsburgh's sudden budget gap reached $28 million; in Detroit the shortfall topped $17 million. One congressional analysis summed up the consequences: "If economic growth does not yield enough State and local tax revenues to replace the phased down anti-recession programs, then certain state and local governments may be forced to raise taxes, cut services, or deplete surplus funds." [4] The staff of the House Budget Committee concluded that national economic recovery will not compensate for the termination of countercyclical aid:

> The fiscal problem at the local level is more likely to be a structural problem resulting from long-run changes in economic activity and population movements rather than economic cycles ... when anti-recession programs are phased down, these problems will persist. [5]

Despite the problems flowing from the program's death, and the appearance of another recession, the push for reenactment of countercyclical aid in 1980 failed as Congress gave new emphasis to limiting the portion of the federal budget devoted to grant programs.

CATEGORICAL GRANTS

Administrative Problems

State and local officials experience many problems in their dealings with categorical grants. At times the problems almost seem to outweigh the obvious financial benefits of the grants. Categorical grants tend to be administered by program experts in the specialized agencies and departments; the explosion in the range of available categorical grants has been accompanied by an apparent increase in the independence of state and program administrators' controls. Also, there seems to be inadequate information on the available categorical grants for use by state and local elected officials. As Elmer Staats, head of the General Accounting Office, told a congressional committee,

> State and local governments must devote considerable time and effort to simply keep informed of available Federal assistance. Because of funding uncertainties associated with many of the programs, available assistance is often learned of too late or offered under time constraints which sometimes preclude states or localities from taking advantage of assistance.[6]

Moreover, the paperwork and red tape associated with grants raise the administrative costs. Federal funding often is uncertain. Finally, regulatory requirements and an excessive number of decision points encourage delay in program implementation.

Paperwork and Red Tape. According to officials of state and local governments, excessive paperwork in both application and reporting requirements permeates the grants system. One reason for this is fragmented federal organization that results in conflict among agencies and inconsistency in procedural requirements. For instance, twelve major economic development programs are housed in five federal agencies. Mayor Kenneth Gibson of Newark, New Jersey, claims that, "Federal urban programs are a nightmare of confusion" and "often are working at cross purposes." Boston's mayor, Kevin White, tells of having to submit 72 applications to nine federal agencies to gain the permits and the resources necessary to revitalize four acres in the downtown area. Local officials recognize that some paperwork is necessary. "We don't object to necessary paperwork," says one official, "even though we grumble and complain. It's the dumb, unnecessary, incomprehensible paperwork that we object to."[7]

Several states are adopting innovations to ease the burden of governmental red tape. A 1976 National Governors' Association report,

Federal Roadblocks to Efficient State Government, documented barriers to effective state program management. A good illustration of this is the fact that in 1976 the Department of Labor required 981 annual submissions of 110 different reports from the Ohio Bureau of Employment Services.

Often federal agencies ask for the same information year after year. In the case of state water pollution control plans, EPA requires annual submissions even when the changes from year to year are minimal. Federal agencies also engage in "overkill," asking for information only indirectly relating to grant purposes. Even more frustrating is the filing of overlapping reports when several agencies need the same information in slightly different forms—as is the case of separate equal opportunity reports for various federal programs.[8]

Paperwork requirements produce other administrative difficulties for the states and localities. The federal grants system reduces state and local productivity levels because of the administrative costs associated with a large number of narrow grant programs. It is a rare federal bureaucrat who thinks twice before asking a state or local agency to complete yet another report.

Funding Uncertainty. Excessive reporting and administrative costs are not the only problems caused by federal practices. For some officials the most troublesome thing about the federal budget is its uncertainty. One state budget officer asserts that "the federal people appropriate anytime around the yearly clock." Timing causes major problems; most states—in fact all but five—and many local governments, enact their budgets by July 1. The federal budget is not determined until October 1. According to Wisconsin's former governor, Patrick Lucey, "under the current system, we are simply engaging in sophisticated guesses as to the level of federal support for federal programs in a given year." This forces states and localities to make frequent last minute adjustments in funding levels that can impair program effectiveness. Faced with this uncertainty, state and local officials now are asking Congress to appropriate funds a year in advance. The prospects are not good for advance funding in many programs—members of Congress, as well as officials in the Office of Management and Budget, want to maintain flexibility and control over programs.[9]

In addition, grants often cause severe cash flow problems. Although formula grants arrive fairly regularly, problems arise if the formulas are updated with current information. Even though officials may know the economic and demographic changes in their jurisdictions, they will lack information on changes in other jurisdictions, thus making their funding estimates unreliable. Also, weeks or months may pass between the time a federal agency allocates the funds and the time the monies are actually available to the states. According to one state budget officer, "such delays may be good for national policy, but they can raise serious problems for program administrators who are operating within tight fiscal constraints and limited appropriations." [10]

Lengthy delays in approval procedures and regulatory clearances are also frequent. Prior to passage of the Community Development Block Grant, it took HUD 31 months to complete the process from application preparation to final award in conventional urban renewal programs. Today the overall review time is reduced to eight months for CDBG awards.[11] EPA's system of dual federal and state review of local wastewater treatment projects, when coupled with environmental reviews for controversial plants, often causes construction delays of several years. This results in significantly higher costs for municipalities which must raise 25 percent of the project's costs.

Regulatory Requirements. Numerous decisions made by state and local governments are constrained by federal requirements which also can prove to be costly. Congress can impose requirements through legislation; the proliferation of policy requirements applied to many grants, and the increased participation of small governments in the intergovernmental grants system mean that constraints now loom as a larger issue. Moreover, inflation, recession, and taxpayer unrest all contribute to emerging criticism of the conditions attached to intergovernmental grants.[12]

In addition to program-specific requirements, Table 6-1 shows that numerous cross-cutting requirements exist. These requirements are enacted in one of two ways: as separate laws applicable to every grant-in-aid, or as separate requirements attached to individual statutes. For example, the Civil Rights Act of 1964 prohibits discrimination in all federally funded activities, and construction grant programs usually contain a clause mandating Davis-Bacon Act requirements for paying prevailing private construction wages. One problem with these requirements is the lack of coordination among the agencies writing regulations. Twenty-eight federal agencies have developed regulations concerning equal access to public buildings and facilities for the handicapped, a requirement of the Rehabilitation Act of 1973.

One complaint about these national policy requirements is that they may divert resources away from a program's substantive goals. Preparation of an environmental impact statement increases the costs of a project and can delay construction. The General Accounting Office recently reported that Davis-Bacon Act prevailing wage requirements add 3.4 percent annually to the cost of federally funded construction projects.[13]

Table 6-1. Major Sources of General Policy Objectives Applicable to Intergovernmental Grant Programs.

Nondiscrimination
Age Discrimination in Employment Act of 1967
Architectural Barriers Act of 1968
Civil Rights Act of 1964, Title VI, VII
Education Amendments of 1972, Title IX
Education for All Handicapped Children Act of 1975
Equal Pay Act of 1963
Executive Orders 11141 (1963) and 1246 (1965), Nondiscrimination in Employment
  By Government Contractors and Subcontractors
Executive Order 11764, Nondiscrimination in Federal Programs, 1968
Executive Order 11914, Nondiscrimination Against the Handicapped, 1976
Rehabilitation Services Act of 1973, Section 504
State and Local Fiscal Assistance Act of 1972
Urban Mass Transportation Act of 1964, as amended 1970, Section 16

Environmental Protection
Clean Air Act of 1970 and Federal Water Pollution Control Act, 1970
Endangered Species Act of 1973
Flood Disaster Protection Act of 1973
National Environmental Policy Act (NEPA), 1969
National Historic Preservation Act of 1966

Planning and Project Coordination
Demonstration Cities and Metropolitan Development Act of 1966
Intergovernmental Cooperation Act of 1968, Title IV

Relocation and Real Property Acquisition
Uniform Relocation Assistance and Real Property Acquisition Policies Act, 1970

Labor and Procurement Standards
Davis-Bacon Act (1931, as incorporated into individual grants)
Office of Federal Procurement Policy Act, 1974
Urban Mass Transportation Act of 1964, as amended, Section 13c
Work Hours Act of 1962

Public Employee Standards
Anti-Kickback (Copeland) Act (1934, 1946, 1960)
Hatch Act (1939, 1940, 1942, 1944, 1946, 1962)
Intergovernmental Personnel Act of 1970

Access to Government Information and Decision Processes
Citizen Participation (numerous grant programs in past three decades)
Family Educational Rights and Privacy Act of 1974 (Buckley Amendment)
Freedom of Information Act, 1974
Privacy Act of 1974

SOURCES: *The Federal Grants Reporter,* National Reporter Systems, 1976; Evelyn Idelson, "1976 Perspective of Title VII," *County News,* April 19, 1976, p. 9; and U.S. Advisory Commission on Intergovernmental Relations, *Categorical Grants: Their Role and Design* (Washington, D.C.: GPO, 1977), p. 235.

While many federal officials acknowledge that regulations are costly, they argue that state and local participation is voluntary. This response begs the question of whether or not more cost effective ways of attaining desired national objectives exist. Even when participation is voluntary, the threat of losing aid often forces grantees into compliance. Furthermore, state and local participation in grant programs is not always voluntary. Several pieces of environmental legislation, such as the Clean Air Act and Federal Water Pollution Control Act, impose sanctions if states and localities do not measure up to national standards. Moreover, the conditions attached to grants-in-aid change over time. The longer a grant program exists, the more political strings will be attached. When Congress adds requirements to programs, many governments see no option but to continue participation. The political costs of denying services to constituents expecting benefits are viewed as too high. The fact that many regulations are applied across-the-board also makes them hard to escape.

Political Impact

Another consequence of categorical grants is the redistribution of political influence within state and local governments. The proliferation of these federal grants during the 1960s and 1970s resulted from intergovernmental alliances between state and local program specialists, federal agencies, interest groups, and legislative staffs. The results have been programs aligned by functional area and controlled by specialists. According to Allen Schick of the Congressional Research Service, "by fostering the establishment of dozens of functional baronies, federal assistance programs undercut the leadership and political capabilities of mayors and governors and contributed to the problems of American cities and states." [14]

Increased Independence of Local Administrators. Legislative and executive control is weakened by the direct links between grant administrators and federal specialists. At the local level the ability of elected officials to influence federal grants is impaired by flow of funds to a wide range of institutions and groups—special districts, housing authorities, community groups, educational institutions, and private firms. One study found that the mayor's office in Tulsa, Oklahoma, underestimated direct federal grants in the city by $27 million due to a lack of information and control. In Tulsa, and in many other areas, public control is weakened by a complex delivery system in which numerous independent actors make decisions using federal funds that have bypassed elected officials. [15]

Even when aid goes directly to agencies under the control of a governor or a mayor, there is still a forging of alliances between the professional administrators in the specialized departments at various levels of government. Federal grants often reduce the ability of elected officials to control public agencies. In fact, in a study conducted of program administrators in eight states, we found that federal grants change the budgetary behavior of state administrators, and that executive and legislative control suffers.[16]

If federal grants insulate state administrators from executive and legislative oversight, one would expect officials in agencies receiving federal aid to exhibit greater independence than officials in unaided agencies. Agency directors often combine two roles. In theory, they are the governor's representatives to the career civil service. They also are expected to speak for and to promote the interests of their agency's constituency. Not surprisingly, agency directors often "join the natives," abandoning the former role for the latter. One measure of loyalty to the governor's program is the frequency of "end runs" or direct appeals to state legislators for more funds than recommended by the governor. In our survey of program administrators, we found that state bureaucrats view executive control over their activities as tenuous. Officials in federally aided agencies appear far more independent of gubernatorial influence than those in other agencies— approximately 38 percent of the unaided officials lobbied for legislative supplements to the executive budget, compared with approximately 60 percent of those receiving federal money.

Federal grants appear to insulate state administrators from state political controls. Professionals in federally-aided agencies mobilize sophisticated intergovernmental allies to support their budget requests. Moreover, state officials often offer interpretations of federal regulations and programs that leave the elected executives with no alternatives. According to an earlier study by Harold Seidman, a former federal management expert, state officials often "were misinterpreting Federal regulations as a means of negating directives promulgated by central executives."[17] Or perhaps it may be that federally aided programs receive less favorable treatment from governors, and this lobbying is an effort to obtain sufficient state funding.

Need for Reprogramming and Supplemental Appropriations. Our study of state program administrators uncovered other relationships between federal support and budgetary behavior. Administrative discretion is always exercised in state budgets, but when the amount of federal funds increases, so too does the likelihood of reprogramming or reallocating funds to other programs. Among the respondents to our survey, approximately 56 percent of the represented state agencies without federal funding reprogrammed funds. Yet almost 75 percent of the agencies receiving more than 25 percent of their budget from federal sources reallocated funds during budget execution. Reprogramming or budgetary adjustment are common occurrences, and often are necessary to maintain managerial discretion and meet unforeseen contingencies. The practices increase, however, as federal aid generates new budget accounts; opportunities for financial leverage also grow, by moving specific items between the various accounts. For example, in New York State the Education Department has continued several positions that the state legislature had directed to be abolished by using federal funds to pay these salaries. In other cases the Education Department bypassed legislative mandates through the use of federal funds to augment programs after the legislature reduced the available state funds.[18]

Supplemental appropriations also are an important part of the state budgetary process. Recipients of federal aid do more lobbying than nonfederal aid recipients, so it is not surprising that we found that, in the eight states studied, more than 60 percent of their agencies received supplemental appropriations. When federal funds were not available to a state agency, state officials were more likely to apply supplementals to new programs; federally funded agencies used supplementals more regularly to maintain basic operations. This example suggests that federal money may be used to initiate programs, while state funds sustain programs.

In short, our analysis demonstrated that agencies receiving federal funds are more likely than nonfederally funded agencies to circumvent the traditional sources of state control over administrative actions. This is reflected in lobbying patterns, budget execution, and reliance on supplemental appropriations.

State and Local Oversight

State planning and budgeting offices frequently examine and co-ordinate information on federal and state funding. State legislatures, on the other hand, typically take a close look only at budget requests that make claims on the state's funds. In a survey of 35 state budget directors, the Advisory Commission on Intergovernmental Relations found that in about one-fifth of the states surveyed, the legislature does not appropriate federal grant funds, and in another one-third of the states, the legislature includes only some of the grants in appropriation bills. Furthermore, in states where federal aid is included in state appropriation bills, only one-third prohibit expenditures above the amount appropriated, and three out of four of these states do not establish priorities within formula grants. State legislatures are also at a disadvantage when federal programs do not have matching requirements or they allow a match by an "in-kind" provision of services, which is very difficult to monitor. State legislatures also lose control over the continuous receipt and transfer of federal funds during the interim between legislative sessions.[19]

The role of elected officials in overseeing state agencies does not formally cease when state agencies become dependent on federal funds. We found that state agency directors do, however, perceive an actual decline in central policy supervision when federal funding is available. Agencies receiving funds from only one or two federal patrons are almost evenly split in their evaluations of state program oversight. Yet when state agencies receive financial support from three or more federal agencies, state legislative and executive review are severely weakened. Sixty-one percent of the surveyed officials who worked with agencies with the most diverse intergovernmental relationships concluded that state supervision of federally funded activities was considerably less than the oversight of state-financed programs.

BLOCK GRANTS

Beginning in 1966 and continuing through the early 1970s, Congress enacted several block grants at the request of presidents Johnson, Nixon, and Ford. According to the ACIR, block grants are programs "by which funds are provided chiefly to general purpose governmental units in accordance with a statutory formula for use in a broad functional area largely at the recipient's discretion."[20] Although the block grant share of federal grant outlays amounted to only 11.3 percent in 1980, as shown in Table 6-2, an examination of how they work helps to explain some of the limits of grants reform.

The five block grants—the Partnership for Health Act of 1966, the Omnibus Crime and Safe Streets Act of 1968, the Comprehensive Employment and Training Act of 1973, the Housing and Community Development Act of 1974, and the Title XX (Social Services) amendments to the Social Security Act—share several basic objectives. Table 6-3 illustrates this point. First, the consolidation of existing categorical grants was aimed at achieving greater economy and efficiency. Second, supporters of individual block grants hoped that consolidation would enhance program visibility and generate pressures for program expansion. A third objective was programmatic decentralization. Grant consolidation and reduced administrative requirements would allow state and local officials in general purpose governments to enhance coordination by forging links between formerly separate activities. Finally, local officials were to be given greater discretion in selecting the activities to be funded by block grants.

As an important corollary to decentralization, block grants aimed at restoring the generalist—the elected chief executive, the legislator,

Table 6-2.   Outlays for Federal Grants.

Type of Grant	1972	1975	1977	1979	1980
General Revenue Sharing	—	12.3%	9.9%	8.3%	8.3%
Other General Purpose	1.5	1.8	4.0	2.6	2.3
Broad-Based Grants	8.4	9.3	12.2	13.9	11.3
Categorical Grants	90.1	76.6	73.9	75.2	78.1
Total	100.0%	100.0%	100.0%	100.0%	100.0%

SOURCE: U.S., Office of Management and Budget, *The Budget for Fiscal Year 1980 Special Analysis* (Washington, D.C.: U.S. Government Printing Office, 1980), p. 230.

and the administrative generalist—to a position of influence over the functional specialists and interest groups that tend to dominate narrow purpose categorical programs.

Significant political and administrative changes followed implementation of the block grant program. As a general rule, the block grants have resulted in greater economy and efficiency. Paperwork costs were reduced, and in many cases the time required for federal grant review was cut greatly. Despite this simplification of grants administration, the full potential of the block grant concept has not been realized. One reason for this is that the block grants may not fully cover a functional area. In the case of the community development block grants, two major HUD programs—the housing rehabilitation loan program and the comprehensive planning and management assistance program—were not included even though they were closely related. Enhanced grantee economy and efficiency is also limited because Congress refused to fold other community development programs administered by the Farmers Home Administration, the Economic Development Administration, and the Appalachian Regional Commission into the block grant.

The ability of state and local governments to achieve substantial savings in block grant administration also is compromised when Congress engages in categorization or recategorization of block grants. According to the ACIR, this occurs when Congress earmarks funds for specific purposes within the block grant framework. In 1971, for example, Congress added to the Safe Streets Act a requirement that 15 to 20 percent of the total block grant allocation be awarded to correctional institutions. In later years Congress added increasing programmatic requirements that limited recipient flexibility. In other block grants the potential for greater efficiency was limited because the block grant approach initially was not fully implemented. For example, 17 categorical programs were consolidated in Title I of CETA, but funds for several special purpose grants—the Job Corps; emergency employment; public service jobs; and programs for seasonal workers, Indians, and youth—were earmarked by the CETA legislation, allowing several categorical programs to continue in the block grant framework.

A second objective of many block grant sponsors was program expansion. In theory, grant consolidation would enhance visibility and tend to cluster support around the broad program. In fact, the block grants as a group have barely held their own in the struggle for a share of the total federal grants outlay. According to one OMB analysis, the block grant share of outlays for federal grants dropped from 13.9 percent in FY 1979 to 11.3 percent in FY 1980.[21]

Political support for categorical grants has proved to be stronger than that for the block grants. Indeed, many groups have pressured Congress to give them greater funding certainty by earmarking funds for certain purposes within the block grant. The weak congressional support for the block grant concept becomes obvious when Congress enacts new categorical grants that logically could have been folded into a block grant. Since 1967, for example, Congress has enacted over a dozen new programs that might have been established under the Partnership for Health Act.[22]

The block grants also aim at decentralizing significant decision-making authority over the use of grant funds by giving the receiving jurisdictions greater discretion in setting program priorities. It is in this area that block grants have registered their greatest success. Although the federal role is greater in some block grants—such as the Safe Streets Act—than in others, as a general rule the broad functional scope of the aid has allowed state and local governments to mesh federal assistance and local priorities. Block grants place greater responsibility on state and local governments to tailor federal assistance to meet local needs.

One study of eight local governments found that block grants gave local jurisdictions new opportunities to coordinate federal grants from below. According to Catherine H. Lovell, ". . . block grants are being linked with each other and are being meshed in innovative and diverse ways with federal categorical grants, state grants, and the jurisdictions' own funds, both public and private, to finance projects tailored to meet specific community needs."[23] Rochester, New York, for example, has established multi-service centers by linking Community Development Block Grant funds and CETA funds for renovation of facilities with various other grant funds that pay for the services provided in the new service centers.

Table 6-3. Structural and Fiscal Characteristics of Contemporary Block Grant Programs, 1977.

Program	Year of Enactment	Number of Categorical Programs Consolidated	Distribution Formula	Primary Recipient	Matching Requirements	Maintenance of Effort Requirements
Partnership for Health	1966	9	population	states	none	no
Omnibus Crime Control and Safe Streets [a]	1968	0	population	states	90-10 (planning) 50-50 (construction) 90-10 (other "action" programs)	yes
Comprehensive Employment and Training [b]	1973	17	unemployment, previous year funding level, low income	general purpose local units and states	none	no
Housing and Community Development [c]	1974	6 [d]	population, housing overcrowding, poverty	general purpose local units	none	yes
Title XX Social Services	1974	0	population	states	90-10 (family planning) 75-25 (other social service programs)	no

[a] Excludes Part C discretionary Grants and Part E (corrections) formula and discretionary grants.
[b] Excludes public service and emergency employment programs.
[c] Excludes outlays for urban renewal and the phase of the other categorical programs replaced by the block grant.
[d] A seventh program, Section 312 Housing Rehabilitation Loans, was also initially proposed for consolidation.

SOURCE: U.S. Advisory Commission on Intergovernmental Relations, *Block Grants: A Comparative Analysis* (Washington, D.C.: U.S. Government Printing Office, 1977), p. 7.

Another indicator of this decentralization appears when grant recipients choose to spend block grant monies in ways that differ from the expenditures made under the old categorical programs. One study finds that while both low- and high-income neighborhoods not funded under categorical community development programs have been included in HUD block grant plans, an even larger number of middle class neighborhoods have been funded.[24] Thus, there is a locally initiated shift in the use of HUD funds away from low-income neighborhoods that reflects an emphasis on neighborhood preservation and growth at the expense of poorer neighborhoods.

A fourth block grant goal is to enhance generalist control over the grants decisionmaking process. In many cases chief executives, legislators, and top administrators are reluctant to get involved. Exceptions appear in those areas, such as community development, where the funds are substantial and the outcomes visible. In other areas—such as health, criminal justice, and manpower—generalists often choose to leave block grant decisionmaking to the experts. For example, although the Safe Streets Act gives governors numerous formal responsibilities, most state chief executives do not spend much time on crime control grant programs. Other demands on the governor's time, as well as the relatively small amount of discretionary funds available, contribute to this limited gubernatorial participation.[25] At the local level, where elected officials may occupy parttime posts, it is even more difficult for elected officials to dominate the decision-making process in relation to block grants.

In summary, block grants exist as a limited alternative to categorical grants. Because they account for less than 12 percent of federal grant outlays, and do not embrace all grants in a single functional area, block grants have done little to simplify grant-in-aid administration. Although state and local governments can now practice "coordination from below" in a limited sphere, the major benefits of block grants—economy, efficiency, program expansion, and generalist control—have not fully materialized. One reason is the tendency toward recategorization and adding strings to block grants, which clearly demonstrates the power of program specialists in intergovernmental relations.

GENERAL REVENUE SHARING

General revenue sharing is by far the most popular program with state and local elected officials. In 1972, when it was enacted, revenue sharing was hailed as a new approach to intergovernmental relations. As one of President Nixon's major domestic policy initiatives, it attempted to restore the authority of elected officials by providing an alternative to the narrow categorical grants programs so often controlled by program specialists.

In fact, no single federal grant program has such strong support among elected state and local officials. In 1972, 1976, and 1980, a strong coalition of state, county, and municipal officials succeeded in overcoming strong congressional opposition to the program. The political decentralization that accompanies the program is one reason for its unpopularity among members of Congress. Critics have maintained that Congress should not appropriate money without retaining control over how it is spent. One of the most outspoken opponents of the program, Representative Jack Brooks of Texas, asserts that, "...revenue sharing is a badly conceived program in which Congress has abdicated its responsibilities and its control over federal expenditures." Even supporters of the program recognize that it is difficult to reconcile the program's two competing objectives—political decentralization and fiscal accountability. Representative Barber Conable of New York, who supports the program, has said that "...there are still members of this body who did not appreciate revenue sharing because little power goes with the grant of revenue sharing money to states and localities." [26]

Although state and local lobbyists have been able to persuade Congress to reauthorize revenue sharing programs both in 1976 and 1980, members who oppose the program have been able to prevent its growth. In fiscal 1975, $6.2 billion was set aside for revenue sharing; in fiscal 1979 revenue sharing entitlements had increased only marginally, to $6.85 billion. As Table 6-2 shows, general revenue sharing accounted for 12.3 percent of federal grant outlays in 1975, but only 8.3 percent in 1980.

It is ironic that the popularity of revenue sharing has not grown in Congress as complaints over federal control and regulation increase. Through 1980, the narrow categorical grants have been more successful than revenue sharing or the block grants in resisting budget cuts. Congress has refused to extend many of the programs funded under one block grant, the Crime Control and Safe Streets Act, and CETA, another block grant, is targeted for budget cuts in 1981 by President Reagan's new director of the Office of Management and Budget. While revenue sharing was reauthorized in late 1980 for an additional three years, it was only after a long battle over the continued participation of the state governments in the program.

Congress came very close to eliminating state government participation from the program in 1980. Some members of Congress supported revenue sharing reauthorization only for localities. Because many states had budget surpluses, or had reduced taxes in recent years, many members of Congress claimed that the federal government needed the revenue sharing funds far more than the states. Local public interest groups joined the governors in pressing for an extension of the state portion of revenue sharing. Both groups were aware that between 25 percent and 40 percent of all the revenue sharing money that went to the states was passed through to local jurisdictions.[27] In November 1980, a compromise was reached, reauthorizing revenue sharing for three years. While the states are excluded from the program during the first year, they are assured participation in the following two years. This shaky compromise indicates that support for revenue sharing among state and local elected officials apparently does not match the intense, if narrow, constituency support behind some of the categorical programs.

FUNGIBILITY AND REALLOCATION

Congress frequently uses categorical and block grants to encourage new programs or to shift state and local priorities. Yet several characteristics of federal administration limit the effectiveness of controlling state and local behavior regarding substantive issues through the use of the grants system. The proliferation of grants creates a confusing intergovernmental maze. Federal agencies frequently use grants to build client relationships with the grant recipients, which impedes strong oversight of state and local operations. The pressures to distribute grants to a broad spectrum of recipients undermines the ability of the regulatory agencies to maintain firm control over a grant program. Moreover, numerous factors, such as the number and scope of grants received by jurisdictions, increase grantee discretion. Often a grantee's discretion increases to the degree that funds are used for purposes other than those authorized. A grant is said to be *fungible* when the state or local government is able to use the grant for purposes other than those intended by Congress. When an agency receives a large grant, it may be able to use the federal funds to substitute for state or local monies.

The proliferation of grants within any given functional area erodes federal control over the uses of each grant. Individually, grants-in-aid may effectively promote national program goals. Yet the steady increase in the number of grants may be self-defeating from the standpoint of effective oversight.

State or local agency directors can pick and choose among grants from several federal agencies; they actually may be accountable to none of their patrons. Fig. 6-1 shows that the vertical links in the federal system are complex and sprawling, rather than clearcut and straightforward. In Missouri, for example, the Division of Family Services receives at least nine federal grants. Comptroller General Staats outlined these complex social service delivery systems before a congressional subcommittee in 1976: 17 federal programs provided funds for manpower services to the disadvantaged, 7 federal programs provided for health services in out-patient health centers, and 11 federal programs funded childcare activities.[28]

Since a one-to-one relationship does not always exist between funding and funded agencies, it may be difficult for federal agencies to monitor state and local activities. They can, at best, only monitor their piece of the action. If state or local agencies receive funds from numerous sources, perhaps no one patron maintains control. State and local agency directors, then, gain more autonomy over policy and programming than suggested by traditional models of national control over grant administration.

Furthermore, in large formula-based grants there are problems in determining how federal funds are spent. When GAO studied the impact of antirecession grants on 15 state governments, it found that "the interchangeable nature of monies, shifting priorities and needs, changing revenue amounts from various sources, and the rel-

Fig. 6-1. Child-Care Activities in the District of Columbia.

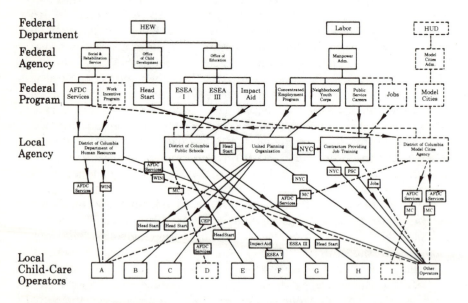

SOURCE: U.S., Senate, Committee on Government Operations, Subcommittee on Intergovernmental Relations, *Government Economy and Spending Reform Act of 1976, Hearings,* 94th Cong., 2d sess., 1976, p. 170.

atively small contribution antirecession payments made to the States' resources impaired analysis of the effect on State budgets." [29] Similarly, a team of investigators expressed doubts about the accuracy of general revenue sharing data collected by the Department of the Treasury: "The differences revealed by this special study of the programmatic impact of revenue sharing clearly indicate that revenue sharing funds have not gone for new public safety and law enforcement programs in anything like the amounts suggested by the ORS (Office of Revenue Sharing) actual-use data." [30]

Although Congress often calls for additional state and local expenditures in an area already funded by a grant, the degree to which federal aid stimulates new expenditures varies. The stimulative effect is greater for project grants than for formula programs (regardless of whether they are block grants or categorical grants) because they are used to encourage recipients to enter new areas. Nonetheless, in many formula categorical and block grant programs, substitution effects are great because no easy or effective way of tracking the use of federal funds exists. The CETA program funds are used by many state and local governments to finance programs they otherwise would have provided on their own. Contrary to legislative intent, many cities, counties, and states did not use the CETA money to hire additional disadvantaged workers. Instead, many jurisdictions became "hooked on CETA" and have used the funds to pay for existing jobs once paid for by local taxes. The head of Boston's CETA agency has said: "Substitution? We do it. Of course we do it. Congress has to understand that this is one of the things propping up big cities these days? "[31] Studies show that four old jobs are financed for every new one created. Additionally, only a fraction of CETA workers are eventually placed in permanent positions. Controls on the program were tightened during the 1978 CETA reauthorization process only after Congress became concerned that the CETA program was becoming a *de facto* form of revenue sharing.[32]

Other factors add to local government discretion in administering federal assistance programs. Almost 40 percent of the categorical grant programs funded in fiscal year 1975 lacked matching funds requirements. In another 11 percent of the grants the required match amounted to no more than 10 percent of eligible costs. In expensive federal programs such as mass transit, however, a low percentage match can still represent a sizeable portion of the state or local budget. It is primarily in the smaller categorical grants programs that matching requirements are lacking.

Maintenance of effort requirements stipulate that state and local governments not reduce their support for a program once a grant is received. The impact of matching funds and maintenance of effort requirements often is softened by arrangements that give grantees latitude in conforming to the federal rules. One GAO study of grants to California found matching requirements in 32 of the 52 programs they investigated, but in 23 grant programs "in-kind" resources, such as volunteer time, are used as alternatives to a cash match. These matches are difficult to monitor and provide great leeway to program administrators. Additionally, some programs—general revenue sharing, the community development block grant and some Farmer's Home Administration programs—can be used to match other federal programs. In 20 of the 32 programs requiring matching funds studied by GAO in California, grants to the state were passed through to localities. Yet in all but two of these grants, the match took place at the aggregate level for the state—relieving each locality of the responsibility for providing a minimum contribution.[33]

Similarly, mitigating factors often reduce the effectiveness of controls imposed by maintenance of effort requirements. In 15 of 37 programs with maintenance of effort mandates studied by GAO in California, federal officials could waive the maintenance of effort requirement under certain conditions. In other programs the base period is outdated, often over a decade old, and inflation lessens its impact on grantee behavior. Finally, in only half the programs can the federal government apply sanctions more stringent than a one-for-one reduction in federal funds because of state or local matching fund shortfalls.

In summary, all types of federal aid are fungible or substitutable to some degree. The degree of substitution depends on several factors. First are the preferences of local or state political officials. Second, federal control over procedural matters frequently is greater than over substantive issues. Third, local governments will exercise greater discretion over broader grants. When the range of permissible uses is broad, as in general revenue sharing or block grants, the ability of federal actors to ensure compliance is more limited than in the narrower categorical grants. Fourth, low matching requirements in many small categorical grant programs now allow state and local governments to participate in some assistance programs without greatly altering their behavior. According to the ACIR fungibility takes place when "the recipient receives a multitude of intergovernmental fiscal transfers, has a number of independent revenue sources, and provides an expanding or broad range of public services."[34]

REGIONAL PLANNING ORGANIZATIONS

In the late 1960s and early 1970s regional planning organizations became a major factor influencing grant program implementation.

In part, this movement was in response to congressional concern about weak local government, fragmentation, and inadequate service delivery. Several federal grant programs enacted during this time included regional planning requirements. For example, Section 208 of the Water Pollution Control Act of 1972 established requirements for regional or areawide planning agencies to develop and implement plans for pollution abatement.

The federal push for regional planning reflects the social, fiscal, and economic realities in urban areas. There was a proliferation of political jurisdictions in the United States in the post-World War II era, particularly in metropolitan areas. This balkanization of governments has led to a splintering of tax resources available to metropolitan areas. Often poor jurisdictions, with disproportionately high levels of social need, are left with insufficient resources. Some governments are not designed to solve the problems of the poor, other governments lack the resources, and the resource-rich jurisdictions often do not have the costly problems to solve.

One solution to the problems associated with political fragmentation—metropolitan government—has not proven acceptable to central city residents or residents of the surrounding suburbs. Suburban residents are unwilling to accept the problems and taxes of the city as their own. In the cities, political elites, especially minority members, fear that metropolitan government will dissipate their power and influence by absorbing city government into larger and whiter jurisdictions just as the minorities are obtaining political power and control over the cities. Certainly none of the nation's leading black mayors—Richard Hatcher (Gary, Ind.), Maynard Jackson (Atlanta), Coleman Young (Detroit), or Tom Bradley (Los Angeles)—is an advocate of metropolitan government.

Alternatively, federal laws and grants have encouraged the proliferation of regional agencies to serve as forums for representatives of governments in urban areas. Councils of Government (COGs), voluntary associations of local governments, can function as planning agencies for the urban area, as organizations responsible for A-95 review and comment on grant applications, as forums for policy resolution, and as vehicles for cooperative implementation of inter-jurisdictional projects. Often COGs and other regional groups, largely assisted by federal grants, evolve from narrow purpose confederations into important intergovernmental actors.

The number of federally supported areawide organizations continues to grow. In 1964 only five grant programs used an areawide approach. In 1972, however, a congressional study reported that over 4,000 regional bodies existed under 24 different federal programs. This raises several troubling points about administrative federalism.

In fact, much of the federally assisted regional or areawide planning actually contributes to fragmentation. Many federal agencies ignore the designated comprehensive planning agency; instead they may set up a separate agency for a slightly different geographic area. Furthermore, according to GAO, areawide programs were "initiated haphazardly over a period of years to satisfy particular needs or demands, not by an interrelated systems approach." Federal agencies also have varying requirements which create impediments and make it difficult for one planning organization to satisfy all federal requirements.[35]

Another result of regional planning is that it engenders power struggles among levels of governments. More importantly, under the guise of supporting decentralized governments close to the people, regional planning and grants delivery become even more complex, confusing, and obscure. As a result, governors, mayors, and county executives often don't know how much federal money is spent in their jurisdiction. One study of federal aid to a typical county, Montgomery County, Ohio, required four years to track down federal aid to agencies in the county. Not only did this study uncover duplication of functions, it showed that $250 million in federal aid was spent in ways that often were at cross purposes. The data also demonstrated that special-purpose governments are six times more dependent on federal funds than state funds. "There is no question that a great many of the special districts are a direct result of federal requirements," said a local planner. Yet this directly contradicts federal policy of favoring general-purpose governments over special districts such as hospital authorities, transit agencies, flood control districts, or sewer authorities.[36]

The present pattern of aid to state and local agencies frustrates the ability of broad governmental units to devise comprehensive plans for community problems. For every effort to support regional planning and large general-purpose governments, several more programs promote functional separation and direct aid to small units. Most counties, cities, and states follow the pattern of Ohio's Montgomery County. They work with only a few pieces of the intergovernmental puzzle. The director of the Montgomery County study concluded: "The hard reality is that in no American community do governmental officials and civic leaders even know the total volume of governmental funds expended, much less how different pieces of the whole are involved in the same problem areas, and to what extent." [37]

CONCLUSIONS

It is the responsibility of state and local officials to implement many federal programs. Definitions of the public interest often differ because officials at different levels of government have varied perspectives. National plans seldom are self-executing and the conditions on which plans are based are rarely static. Traditionally, the grants process is seen as a mechanism for resource allocation by the federal government. In fact, however, officials in larger jurisdictions often pick and choose among federal programs. Frequently they simply use federal funds to fulfill their own priorities, by playing one federal agency against another, or by manipulating the various restrictions placed on their income by the federal government. In larger jurisdictions, which qualify for a number of federal programs, a good deal of fungibility or co-mingling of funds exists. In some cases federal funds actually are used as the state or local matching share to attract additional federal dollars. Intergovernmental administration, then, involves resource mobilization by grant recipients as well as resource allocation by the grantor agency.

This does not mean that federal grants do not alter the behavior of subnational governments. Federal grants often force changes in administrative structure, civil service laws, and areas such as affirmative action practices. Grants-in-aid also stimulate many governments to expand their activities and develop new programs. Yet, the complexity of the federal aid system also has weakened the control of elected officials by lengthening the lead times necessary for action and by multiplying the number of clearance and decision points. Given these conditions, along with the influence that the subnational governments exert at earlier stages in the policy process, there has been a tendency on the part of the grantees to sustain environments in which they can influence conditions that will enhance their goals.

Once program administration begins, program specialists can sustain relative independence from the elected officials. It is the complexities of the intergovernmental grants system in a federal union that causes this independence of political controls over all federal grants programs. Efforts to arrest this condition, such as block grants, have barely dented the functionally oriented categorical grants system, and recent developments continue to undermine control of grants management by elected officials at all levels. As the number and scope of grant programs continue to grow, federal officials increasingly lose their ability to monitor or control program implementation.

NOTES

1. U.S. Advisory Commission on Intergovernmental Relations, "Federal Initiatives and Impacts," *Intergovernmental Perspective* 4 (Winter 1978): 8.
2. Rochelle L. Stanfield, "Federal Aid for Cities—Is It a Mixed Blessing?" *National Journal* 10 (June 3, 1978): 869-870.

3. John Herbers, "U.S. Aid Contradicts Tulsa's Image of Independence," *New York Times,* April 2, 1979, p. 10.

4. U.S., House of Representatives, Committee on the Budget, *Phasing Down Antirecession Programs: Fiscal Year 1979 Budget Issues* (Washington, D.C.: U.S. Government Printing Office, 1978), p. 10.

5. Ibid., p. 15.

6. U.S., Senate, Committee on Government Operations, *Hearings: Government Economy and Spending Reform Act of 1976* (Washington, D.C.: U.S. Government Printing Office, 1976), p. 157.

7. Ronald G. Shafer, "Red Tape is Hobbling Federal Benefit Programs and Raising Costs, State and Local Officials Say," *Wall Street Journal,* May 4, 1977.

8. Rochelle L. Stanfield, "States are Fighting Their Way Out of a Federal Paperwork Bag," *National Journal* 8 (September 25, 1976): 1344-1346; and National Governors' Conference, *Federal Roadblocks to Efficient State Government* (Washington, D.C.: National Governors' Conference, 1977).

9. Rochelle L. Stanfield, "State and Local Governments Favor the Pay-in-Advance Plan," *National Journal* 9 (March 5, 1977): 348-351.

10. S. Kenneth Howard, "Federal Grants: Their Impact on State Budget Offices," *State Government* 50 (Spring 1977): 98.

11. U.S. Advisory Commission on Intergovernmental Relations, *Community Development: The Workings of a Federal Local Block Grant* (Washington, D.C.: U.S. Government Printing Office, 1977), p. 45.

12. The following section is largely based on the U.S. Advisory Commission on Intergovernmental Relations, *Categorical Grants: Their Role and Design* (Washington, D.C.: U.S. Government Printing Office, 1977), Chapter 7.

13. U.S., General Accounting Office, *The Davis-Bacon Act Should Be Repealed* (Washington, D.C.: U.S. General Accounting Office, 1979) p. 68.

14. Allen Schick, "The Intergovernmental Thicket: The Questions Still are Better than the Answers," *Public Administration Review* 35 (December 1975): 718.

15. Herbers, "U.S. Aid," p. 10.

16. The following section is based on: George E. Hale and Marian Lief Palley, "The Impact of Federal Funds on the State Budgeting Process," *National Civil Review* 67 (November 1978): 461-473.

17. Harold Seidman, *Politics, Position & Power* (New York: Oxford University Press, 1970), p. 155.

18. New York State, Assembly, Ways and Means Committee, *Appropriating Federal Funds: A Proposal for New York State* (Albany, N.Y.: New York State Legislature, 1976), p. iii.

19. U.S. Advisory Commission on Intergovernmental Relations, *The Intergovernmental Grants System as Seen by Local, State, and Federal Officials* (Washington, D.C.: U.S. Government Printing Office, 1977), pp. 101-105.

20. See U.S. Advisory Commission on Intergovernmental Relations, *Block Grants: A Comparative Analysis* (Washington, D.C.: U.S. Government Printing Office, 1977), p. 6.

21. U.S., Office of Management and Budget, *The Budget for Fiscal Year 1980 Special Analysis* (Washington, D.C.: U.S. Government Printing Office, 1979), p. 230.

22. U.S. Advisory Commission on Intergovernmental Relations, *Block Grants,* p. 16.

23. Catherine H. Lovell, "Coordinating Federal Grants from Below," *Public Administration Review* 39 (September/October 1979): 432.
24. Raymond A. Rosenfeld, "Local Implementation Decisions for Community Development Block Grants," *Public Administration Review* 39 (September/October 1979): 448.
25. ACIR, *Block Grants,* p. 28.
26. John Herbers, "End to Federal Revenue Sharing Expected in Forthcoming Budget," *New York Times,* July 10, 1979, p. 16.
27. Dale Tate, "States Face Uphill Battle in Revenue Sharing Debate," *Congressional Quarterly Weekly Report* 39 (February 23, 1980): 531.
28. U.S., Senate, Committee on Government Operations, *Hearings: Government Economy and Spending Reform Act* (Washington, D.C.: U.S. Government Printing Office, 1976), p. 157.
29. U.S., General Accounting Office, *Impact of Antirecession Assistance on 15 State Governments* (Washington, D.C.: U.S. Government Printing Office, 1978), p. ii.
30. U.S. Advisory Commission on Intergovernmental Relations, *Summary and Concluding Observations* (Washington, D.C.: U.S. Government Printing Office, 1978), p. 41.
31. Urban C. Lehner, "Federally Backed CETA Program Grows, But a Few Cities Encounter Problems," *Wall Street Journal,* June 30, 1978.
32. Harrison H. Donnelly, "CETA: Successful Job Program or Subsidy for Local Governments," *Congressional Quarterly Weekly Report* 36 (March 28, 1978): 1-8.
33. U.S. Advisory Commission on Intergovernmental Relations, *Categorical Grants: Their Role and Design* (Washington, D.C.: U.S. Government Printing Office, 1977), p. 111; and U.S., General Accounting Office, *Will Federal Assistance to California Be Affected by Proposition 13?* (Washington, D.C.: U.S. Government Printing Office, 1978), pp. 13-15.
34. ACIR, *Summary and Concluding Observations,* p. 421.
35. U.S., General Accounting Office, *Federally Assisted Areawide Planning Need to Simplify Policies and Practices* (Washington, D.C.: U.S. Government Printing Office, 1977), p. ii.
36. Rochelle L. Stanfield, "The Things Nobody—but Montgomery County, Ohio—Knows," *National Journal* 8 (Dec. 25, 1976): 1811.
37. Ibid., p. 1810.

7

The Impact of Intergovernmental Grants on Urban Areas

To understand the intergovernmental grants process and the application of a regulatory model it will be useful to examine more closely how different kinds of jurisdictions interact within the grants system. In this chapter, we will examine federal grants to urban areas. To identify jurisdictions for the purpose of this analysis, a distinction had to be drawn between that which is *urban* and that which is *rural*. The United States Bureau of the Census defines an urban area as a place that has a population of 2,500 people or more. This definition is not very useful for the purposes of this study. We will treat as urban those jurisdictions with populations of more than 50,000 and smaller towns within a larger Standard Metropolitan Statistical Area.

Urban areas have increasingly become dependent on federal grants, and it is important to understand the reasons, effects, and scope of this dependence. In particular, we will explore the changes in the intergovernmental relationship caused by dependency and its effect on programs and planning.

To understand the impact of the federal grants system and the similarity of the grants process to the regulatory process, we will first consider the current urban condition—particularly the problems caused by the fragmentation of both urban resources and urban services. Another problem is raised by the growth of the Sun Belt population and its economic base and the concurrent population loss and economic decay experienced by the urban areas of the Northeast and Midwest. The federal grants system is being strained by the need to be more responsive to these needs, particularly in the face of the political controversies over which jurisdictions should receive federal funds and over what mechanisms should deliver federal funds to recipient units.

After some contemporary urban problems are discussed, the urban grants process will be examined to better explain the problem of program fragmentation. Finally, the competition between various levels of government will be described. In the following discussion we will consider how and why the grant system performs less as a system and more as a fragmented and unintegrated potpourri of programs.

THE CURRENT URBAN DILEMMAS

Older Cities and Suburbs

There has been a serious deterioration in the economic, fiscal, and social conditions in many of the older cities and suburbs in the United States. Often their governments, in an attempt to stay afloat financially, have requested additional support from the states and the federal government. Adverse conditions have resulted from a variety of conditions, most notably the movement of both industrial employers and the middle class out of the older cities and suburbs into the newer suburban communities. The cities with the worst conditions are clustered in the Northeast. Table 7-1 shows the composite measures of economic, social, and fiscal need for 45 large American cities.

The deterioration of economic, fiscal, and social conditions of cities is associated with the deterioration of city infrastructures. In Cleveland, it has been estimated that it would take an estimated $700 million to bring the roads, sewers, water system, and bridges up to acceptable standards. New York City Deputy Mayor Phillip Trimble reported to the congressional Joint Economic Committee that, "The order of magnitude (of the problem) must simply be horrendous. If you really did a study on a nationwide basis, it would be larger than the defense budget." Local officials nationwide agree that Proposition 13-type tax limits, high interest rates, and inflation have put an unreachable price tag on the maintenance of city structures and have hampered local governments in their efforts to raise capital through taxes or bonds. Cities increasingly have been deferring maintenance of their capital plants—since 1973 Buffalo has cut its maintenance workforce by 42 percent, Philadelphia by 22 percent, and Newark by 21 percent. It is not surprising that many people find these cities difficult places in which to live. Therefore, when they can afford to leave the older central cities and suburbs, many will move to communities that are better maintained.[1]

Table 7-1. Composite Measures of Social, Economic, and Fiscal Need for 45 Cities.

City	Social Need Score	Social Need Rank	Economic Need Score	Economic Need Rank	Fiscal Need Score	Fiscal Need Rank
Northeast						
Albany	NA	—	59	21	28	28
Boston	45	15	74	8	72	2
Buffalo	61	6	77	5	44	13
Jersey City	48	13	78	3	47	8
Newark	100	1	84	1	65	4
New York	41	21	80	2	67	3
Patterson	NA	—	72	9	45	12
Philadelphia	49	12	70	12	53	6
Pittsburgh	43	20	71	10	37	18
Rochester	44	19	70	11	36	19
Midwest						
Akron	37	25	64	17	27	29
Chicago	46	16	76	6	NA	—
Cincinnati	45	17	65	16	44	14
Cleveland	67	2	78	4	42	16
Columbus	34	26	51	28	28	26
Detroit	62	4	66	15	46	9
Gary	58	8	58	22	31	24
Indianapolis	2	35	37	37	22	32
Kansas City	29	30	56	24	NA	—
Milwaukee	37	23	64	18	NA	—
Minneapolis	20	37	62	20	23	31
Oklahoma City	30	29	34	39	NA	—
St. Louis	64	3	74	7	61	5
South						
Atlanta	47	14	45	30	NA	—
Baltimore	55	9	63	19	52	7
Birmingham	51	11	45	31	46	10
Dallas	11	39	35	38	NA	—
El Paso	NA	—	30	41	34	21
Houston	2	34	26	43	NA	—
Louisville	45	18	51	27	35	20
Miami	60	7	42	34	31	23
New Orleans	61	5	53	26	45	11
Norfolk	30	28	40	36	44	15
Tampa	51	10	29	42	29	25
Washington, D.C.	NA	—	54	25	84	1
West						
Anaheim	NA	—	31	40	10	38
Denver	20	36	41	35	33	22
Los Angeles	27	31	57	23	18	34
Phoenix	24	32	16	45	18	33
Sacramento	40	22	43	33	24	30
San Bernadino	NA	—	49	29	28	27
San Diego	30	27	43	32	17	35
San Jose	37	24	24	44	12	37
San Francisco	22	33	68	13	39	17
Seattle	16	38	66	14	13	36

SOURCE: U.S., House of Representatives, Committee on Banking, Finance and Urban Affairs, Subcommittee on the City, *Report: City Need and the Responsiveness of Federal Grants Programs* (Washington, D.C.: GPO, 1978), p. 53.

The Mismatch of Needs and Resources

The exodus of industry and the taxpaying middle class, along with the continuing presence of a disproportionate number of the working poor and unemployed, have made the generation of local revenues very difficult in many cities. In addition to the high cost of services required by the city population—which is disproportionately the very young and the very old—there are costly areawide services that the cities provide. Often these services, such as transportation, are expensive. While the commuter population within the metropolitan area uses them, it does not necessarily share a fair part of the cost.

The problems generated by the need to provide services—schools, recreation, and health care services for the young along with health care services, housing, safety and recreational services for the elderly— are compounded by financial pressures. The city population cannot afford to pay directly for all the services it requires. As these costs have grown, jurisdictions often have raised taxes and fees. As these tax rates and fees have increased, the taxpaying public and businesses have relocated. As people and businesses leave, the taxpaying population shrinks and the burden on those remaining increases—starting the cycle all over again.

Urban Tax Strategies. The most lucrative tax employed by most municipal jurisdictions is the property tax. If a comparable piece of property in a suburban jurisdiction is taxed at a lower rate, people will have a reason to move. Nevertheless, cities rely on this taxing mechanism rather heavily. The reason can be traced to the national and state tax systems. The income tax, the most elastic tax mechanism used by American governments to raise revenues, is the near exclusive tool of the federal and state governments. Consequently, though some local governments have been permitted to impose income taxes—Washington, D.C., and New York City, for example—local governments usually are forced to rely heavily on the inelastic property tax to generate local revenues. Unlike the income tax, where growth is automatic when wages increase, politicians must choose to raise property tax rates or assessments to secure additional revenue. When property tax rates are increased to a level that is unacceptable, city residents may decide to leave the jurisdiction or to elect a new city council.

Where do middle class taxpayers and businesses move when they are dissatisfied with the economic conditions of the city? Often they move into the outlying areas that have developed around the cities. This condition leads to the political balkanization of many metropolitan areas and to the development of another component of the urban problem. Once they have moved into suburban and exurban communities, the middle class does not have to pay for expensive services for the disadvantaged and the elderly, but may still have access to other urban services. For example, hospitals and medical centers traditionally have been located in the older central cities. These complexes often maintain teaching and research facilities and are significant regional resources. Health care professionals affiliated with these institutions may establish offices in the surrounding neighborhoods. In order to support these public, tax-exempt institutions, roads must be maintained, public transportation provided, and public safety guaranteed. Yet the city cannot directly tax the medical center's suburban patients.

Many cities offset this problem by charging nonresidents who work in the city a commuter or wage tax. However, the areawide services provided by the city also are used by people who both live and work outside city limits. This group may not pay to maintain the city services which undergird the regional economy. State and county government complexes, areawide post offices, and university centers, all of which provide regional services, are often located in cities. In addition, cultural and religious facilities, which are used by suburban area residents as well as by city residents, are often located in cities. All of these facilities are exempt from taxation. An extreme example of this condition exists in Newark, New Jersey, where over one-half of the property in the city is not taxable.

Although there has been some movement of the middle class back into some cities, a phenomenon known as *gentrification,* it would be a mistake to overstate the effects of this in-migration on available city tax revenues. According to a Census Bureau analysis in 1978, the median income of central city families was only 70 percent of the median suburban family income. Gentrification does affect the character of sections of cities; often it forces the existing, sometimes poor, segments of the population into other more densely populated areas of the city. Moreover, in most cities the revenue problems have not been solved by this movement, which until 1980 was still quite small.

Federal and State Assistance. Local revenue sources have not been sufficient to meet urban needs, and in many jurisdictions the federal and state governments have moved in to assist urban areas. We will now directly examine the financial plight of the older cities and suburbs.[2]

During the 30 years from 1949 to 1979, state and local revenues increased by more than 1,200 percent from $18 billion to $257.5 billion annually. Although this growth sounds enormous, these funds still fail to meet urban needs and must be supplemented by federal and state economic assistance. In fiscal 1977 intergovernmental sources provided cities with $42.5 billion, a $3.5 billion increase over the previous year. Just over $13.5 billion of these funds came from the federal government; the rest of the transfers came to city governments from the states—either as original tax revenue or as federal money passed through the states to the localities.[3]

Prior to enactment of the general revenue sharing program in 1972, federal funds amounted to approximately 14 percent of all intergovernmental transfers to municipalities, with the states providing the remaining 86 percent of the transfers—which included federal dollars passed through the states to localities. By fiscal 1975 this proportion of federal-state aid had changed to approximately 28 percent federal aid and 72 percent state aid.[4]

The average per capita expenditures in fiscal 1975 for all municipalities was $358.65 with larger jurisdictions having higher per capita expenditures than smaller jurisdictions. Jurisdictions with populations of 1 million or more had average per capita expenditures of $844.44 compared to average per capita expenditures of $193.55 in municipalities with populations of fewer than 50,000. In addition, large municipalities received a larger portion of their revenues from intergovernmental sources than did smaller municipalities, as shown in Table 7-2.

The fiscal plight of the cities has been exacerbated by the impact of the inflation/recession cycle that has plagued the United States in the past decade. Often the first industries to falter when a recession takes hold are the marginal, labor-intensive companies. As these enterprises close their doors, their workers become eligible for welfare programs. These workers, often among the poorest paid of the industrial work force, thus become recipients of public revenues. Furthermore, the local government loses another revenue source as payroll and taxes do not flow into the urban economy at a time when greater demands are being made upon it.

One final point should be noted here. The financial and fiscal strains are compounded in some urban areas by severe social problems. In particular, high crime rates, vandalism, arson, and a lack of social integration have all led to further problems that cities have been especially hard-pressed to solve—despite infusions of state and federal aid.

Competition Between Frost Belt and Sun Belt Cities

The discussion thus far has focused on older suburbs and cities that are located predominantly in the Northeast and Midwest and are afflicted with severe social, fiscal, and financial strains. All urban areas are not so unfortunate as those jurisdictions. More specifically,

Table 7-2. Average Annual Rate of Growth in Per Capita Expenditure, and Selected Other Items, 1962-1975.

City Size	Per Capita Expenditures 1962	Per Capita Expenditures 1975	Annual Average Rate of Growth in Per Capita Expenditures 1962-75	Per Capita Aid 1962	Per Capita Aid 1975	Annual Average Rate of Growth in Per Capita Aid 1962-75	Aid ÷ Own Source Revenue 1962	Aid ÷ Own Source Revenue 1975	Number of Cities 1962	Number of Cities 1975
All municipalities	$113.56	$358.65	9.20%	$22.66	$144.76	15.27%	25.85%	65.10%	—	—
1,000,000+	219.11	844.44	10.89	49.50	437.85	18.22	28.50	90.50	5	6
500,000-999,999	166.49	531.95	9.30	39.53	216.68	13.94	32.23	71.50	17	20
300,000-499,999	124.06	413.96	9.65	25.11	156.07	15.07	27.08	60.76	21	20
200,000-299,999	126.87	395.31	9.05	22.59	153.57	15.83	23.53	64.22	19	17
100,000-199,999	122.73	340.66	8.13	23.24	118.60	13.35	24.43	54.56	68	95
50,000-99,999	111.25	295.62	7.75	19.11	90.76	12.68	22.21	46.55	180	229
Less than 50,000	63.16	193.55	8.98	10.44	62.84	14.75	21.23	47.07	17,690	18,130

SOURCE: U.S. Advisory Commission on Intergovernmental Relations staff computations based on data from U.S., Department of Commerce, Bureau of the Census, *Compendium of City Government Finance in 1962* and U.S., Department of Commerce, Bureau of the Census, *Compendium of City Government Finances in 1975*, various tables.

the urban growth areas disproportionately located in the Southeast and the Southwest are operating with very different fiscal, financial, and social conditions. The urban areas in these regions are generally experiencing economic growth and are not as dependent on state and federal aid as the cities in the Northeast and Midwest. However, these healthy Sun Belt cities are not economically balanced. Despite sufficient revenues for the maintenance of public services without threat of bankruptcy or default, many cities in America's Sun Belt have pockets of poverty and need. When considering the allocation formulas for federal funds to cities, Sun Belt cities tend to favor those mechanisms that provide for fund distribution based on the extent of poverty, overcrowded housing, and total population. The older Frost Belt cities tend to favor formulas that consider the age of housing stock, their loss in population, the number of people living in poverty conditions, and the higher regional cost of living in the Northeast.

Because of these different pressures, splits have arisen between the two groups when urban aid legislation and formulas have been under consideration. Congress may grant administrative agencies some discretion in how the formulas should be applied. For example, the original Community Development and Housing Act permitted HUD to make cost-of-living adjustments in the poverty component of the formula. HUD officials declined, however, to make any adjustments, claiming that the available information was insufficient to alter funds distribution. The effect of this decision was to help Sun Belt cities even though the original legislative formula tended to favor older northeastern and midwestern cities.[5]

The different types of cities favor different formulas for funds distribution. Furthermore, whereas economic and community redevelopment are serious concerns for Frost Belt cities, they are not of central concern to Sun Belt cities. In addition, high energy costs afflict Frost Belt cities as a result of the need for expensive, often imported, home heating fuel. Sun Belt cities require less home heating fuel and are closer to domestic energy sources. Thus the split between Sun Belt and Frost Belt cities persists, reinforced by regional differences in economic growth and development.

THE URBAN GRANTS PROCESS

The proliferation of federal grants to subnational governments was discussed in Chapter 6. At this point, it is instructive to consider specifically how the expansion of the federal grants process affects urban areas, how the funds are channeled to urban areas, and what consequences flow from this new source of urban revenue to American cities and suburbs.

Extent of Aid

The proliferation of grants available to subnational governments has altered the nature of the federal-state-local relationship. Urban jurisdictions now have a new position in the federal relationship as a result of the expansion of grants and the changing patterns of distribution. The programs that provide funds to cities now cross into almost every policy and program area that operates at the city level.

According to John Shannon, an assistant director of the ACIR, the cities are now "creatures of the state but wards of the federal government." Since the mid-1960s cities have begun to look to the federal government directly for funds to build housing, underwrite economic development, and support mass transportation. This federal aid, even the less restrictive revenue sharing and block grants, comes with procedural strings. When the city of Philadelphia wanted to use Department of Transportation categorical grant funds to build a downtown pedestrian walkway, city officials were told that the project had to include a mass transit component to be eligible for this money. Consequently, the Philadelphia Chestnut Street Walkway now has buses operating on it.[6]

The extent of the federal funds that flow into the nation's 48 largest cities is quite substantial. In 1968 it was estimated that of the $11.8 billion spent in these cities, 5.6 percent came from federal grants. Ten years later, in 1978, of the $38.1 billion expended in these cities it was estimated that 18.4 percent was federally derived. Put into a somewhat different focus, the ACIR estimated that in 1957, for every $1 raised locally in 47 of the nation's largest cities (excluding New York City), these cities received $.02 from federal government sources. In 1978 the comparable figure was estimated to be $.50 from federal sources. The impact of these funds varies among cities. Detroit, in 1978, received $.64 from the federal government for every dollar it raised locally. Cleveland received $.68, Buffalo received $.62, and Milwaukee received $.61.[7] Problems arise when these data are used to compare the dependence of various cities on federal aid. Not all local governments are responsible for the same services. What is clear from these data, however, is that cities are more dependent on federal dollars than ever before in our history and that federal intrusion into urban politics is a fact of life.

No one knows exactly how much federal money flows directly into any American city in any given year. In part this is because direct federal aid is only a small portion of the federal money that actually reaches the cities. Large sums of money are funneled through state governments for welfare, education, sewer construction, crime control, and other programs. Funds also go to the special districts that often provide services to urban areas. Federal aid for education goes directly to school districts, for example. If the school district is an independent district and not part of the city, the funds from the Elementary and Secondary Education Act (ESEA) will not appear as city revenues received.

The variety of mechanisms available for the channeling of federal grants dollars into urban areas often makes it very difficult to facilitate comprehensive planning. The problems that can arise regarding planning for school programs and work training programs illustrate this point. The federal education programs are funded largely by ESEA; the federal work programs are funded to a considerable extent by the Comprehensive Employment and Training Act (CETA). The ESEA funds go to school districts; the manpower money flows to municipalities or counties. To plan and coordinate educational programs and job training programs, it is necessary to bring together officials from two separate jurisdictions, each with their own constituencies and interests to protect. Another example of coordination problems is the Department of Energy's weatherization program, in which direct grants go to independent community action agencies (CAAs). Yet Energy Department regulations require that CETA funds be used to provide the weatherization workforce. This requires close cooperation between the CAAs and the CETA prime sponsor. Coordination of programming under such circumstances may be difficult.

Types of Programs

Though a multitude of grant programs are in place to assist in the delivery of urban services, most of the funds come from very few sources. In fiscal 1978, state and federal intergovernmental aid to *all* local governments amounted to approximately $85.5 billion; $20.5 billion was in the form of direct federal aid, $15 billion was indirect federal aid (passed through the state) and $50 billion was direct state aid.[8] Nineteen billion of the federal dollars were channeled to local jurisdictions (largely urban special districts and general purpose governments) from just five programs. These programs included general revenue sharing, antirecession fiscal assistance, Community Development Block Grants, the Labor Department's CETA program, and the Commerce Department's local public works grants. These five programs, all broad in purpose, offered considerable discretion to local offices regarding program content.[9] Reliance upon these five grants varied from jurisdiction to jurisdiction, but the extent of

Table 7-3. Composition of Federal Grants, Selected Cities Fiscal Year 1978 (*thousands of dollars*).

City	Public Service Employment (CETA)	Local Public Works	Anti-Recession Fiscal Assistance	Community Development Block Grant	Other (Including General Revenue Sharing)	Stimulus Package and CDBG as % of Total
Northern						
Boston	$ 21,532	$ 15,963	$ 7,599	$ 25,235	$ 47,768	59.6%
Buffalo	17,378	13,495	5,739	21,928	20,121	74.4
Chicago	69,248	37,483	22,287	116,800	152,538	61.7
Detroit	39,242	26,805	25,158	57,778	162,563	47.8
Indianapolis	17,158	10,575	3,154	10,941	29,503	58.6
Minneapolis	10,800	7,394	1,619	18,625	17,044	69.3
New York	198,612	191,903	143,117	224,775	490,048	60.7
Philadelphia	42,820	54,734	30,834	63,852	137,877	58.2
Pittsburgh	12,900	16,242	7,162	23,815	32,733	64.7
St. Louis	16,074	15,514	9,681	32,983	35,131	67.9
Southern & Western						
Atlanta	18,078	7,205	2,625	14,125	13,060	76.3
Dallas	8,172	0	0	15,223	16,465	58.7
Denver	9,402	8,527	3,135	11,572	30,287	51.9
Houston	16,646	8,650	1,588	23,634	131,866	61.3
Los Angeles	78,792	45,794	15,585	51,010	95,513	66.7
Nashville	4,596	0	0	8,510	23,323	36.0
New Orleans	11,612	9,508	7,172	20,287	36,768	56.9
Phoenix	22,572	15,335	2,390	10,031	15,306	76.7
San Francisco	25,264	30,030	9,529	26,335	70,962	56.2

SOURCE: George E. Peterson and Thomas Muller, *The Regional Impact of Federal Tax and Spending Policies* (Washington, D.C.: The Urban Institute, 1977), p. 29.

big city reliance upon these grants can be demonstrated readily by examining Table 7-3.

Although the public works and the antirecession grants were not renewed in 1979 or in 1980, the remaining three large broad-based programs still allowed urban jurisdictions flexibility and discretion regarding the spending of their federal funds; revenue sharing places no restrictions on expenditures. As a result, these monies tend to be used for a wide variety of purposes by most urban jurisdictions. Richard P. Nathan and Charles F. Adams provide some information on the ways in which revenue sharing funds have been spent. On the basis of expenditure patterns in 29 cities, as well as several other types of jurisdictions, they found that smaller cities used 75 percent of their revenue sharing allotments for expansion programs (especially construction projects). Cities with populations of more than 100,000 used over 50 percent of their allocations to hold down taxes or to avoid borrowing.[10] Table 7-4 presents some interesting data on the actual expenditure patterns by program area.

Some Differences Among the Grant Programs

Not all of the federal grant dollars that flow into urban jurisdictions go to local governments to use in their programs. Substantial federal grants money flows to individuals through the states. In particular, two federal grants programs, intended to provide health assistance and income security, are directed to individuals. Aid to Families with Dependent Children (AFDC) and Medicaid (financial aid to the "medically indigent" for health care services) are the major components of these grants areas. These two programs are framed as categorical-formula grants to states. The states must provide some matching funds—determined by a formula—to be eligible to receive the federal dollars. The states set up their own eligibility requirements within federal guidelines and provide assistance to those eligible. In some states the nonfederal share of the program is paid in part by the state and in part by the counties. For example, in New York State, New York City must cover approximately 20 percent of the total AFDC costs. The burden of the nonfederal share of these programs not funded by the states can be very large. In New York State the typical urban county devotes over 50 percent of its operating budget to AFDC and Medicaid payments.

Although these grants to individuals—who often reside in urban jurisdictions—are included in the total dollar value of federal grants to urban areas, it could be argued that this is an inaccurate cost accounting. The urban jurisdictions themselves receive federal dollars to a lesser extent than inclusion of these programs into the total lead one to believe. When AFDC and Medicaid recipients move from

Table 7-4. Revenue Sharing Expenditures by State and Local Governments Reported to the Bureau of the Census, 1976-1977.

Category	Actual Expenditures (thousands of dollars)	Percent
Airport	7,963	0.1
Corrections	166,652	2.5
Education	1,248,437	19.0
Finance/general administration	327,675	5.0
Fire protection	523,467	8.0
General public spending	261,719	4.0
Health	476,732	7.3
Highways	799,024	12.2
Hospitals	138,542	2.1
Housing/urban renewal	17,627	0.3
Interest and general debt	55,811	0.9
Libraries	79,722	1.2
Natural resources	27,455	0.4
Parks and recreation	247,588	3.8
Police protection	942,809	14.4
Public welfare	165,699	2.5
Redemption of debt	90,214	1.4
Sanitation and sewerage	370,877	5.7
Utility systems	79,281	1.2
Others	527,400	8.0
Total	6,554,694	100.0

SOURCE: U.S., Department of the Treasury, Office of Revenue Sharing (Washington, D.C.: U.S. Government Printing Office, 1979), p. 8.

urban to suburban or rural jurisdictions within the same state, they will continue to receive these payments if their income level does not change. Thus, if the extent of federal aid to urban jurisdictions is reestimated for fiscal 1979, such that the portion of the $12.3 billion federal contribution to Medicaid and the $6.7 billion contribution to AFDC that goes to urban residents is subtracted from the total, the dependence of cities on federal aid will not seem as great.

Effects of Grants on Urban Resource Bases

When the federal dollars channeled into urban areas come from block grants or general revenue sharing, there is no *immediate* cost for the receiving jurisdiction. However, when the revenue sources are categorical grants, there is often a local matching funds requirement. This can cause fiscal problems. In addition, any project grant that sets up a program or assists in the construction of a project leaves the recipient jurisdiction with the costs of continuing the program and/or the costs of maintaining the project. Thus, when the federal government provides funding under the Urban Mass Transportation Administration (UMTA) for subway systems, the receiving jurisdiction must provide a local match of 10 percent of the federal contribution. Once the facility is in place, the local jurisdictions are responsible for maintenance and personnel. Thus, through the largesse of the federal government urban jurisdictions have acquired new expenses.

Rising hospital costs have been caused, in part, by the nature of federal aid. The Hill-Burton Act funded categorical grants for hospital construction, which allowed many jurisdictions to expand existing facilities or to build new facilities. Once these institutions were in place, the costs of maintaining them became a local concern. In some jurisdictions, the local government has helped cover some of the costs—particularly capital maintenance costs. Several federal programs, especially Medicare and Medicaid, help patients to pay their hospital bills; many urban hospitals have, therefore, expanded to meet the need. However, they have had to pass the costs along to the patients.

Problems and Costs of Compliance

All federal grants, even the less restrictive types of grants, require that receiving agencies or jurisdictions comply with certain regulations reflecting national policy goals. Noncompliance can result in withdrawal of federal funds, but the costs of compliance must be covered by the recipient of the funds.

The costs associated with environmental impact studies are incurred locally, for example. The costs associated with developing and maintaining affirmative action programs are also local. In addition to these regulations, all federal grants have specific federal regulations for implementation with which a recipient government is expected to comply. Before a block grant application can be submitted to HUD, a city must certify that 13 general requirements have been met. These requirements include citizen participation, equal employment opportunity, and an environmental assessment, among others. Even relatively simple tasks are subjected to these requirements. According to A. Howe Todd, the assistant manager of the city of Richmond, Virginia, ". . . before we can plant trees in a development area, we have to go through the whole environmental assessment, complete with the newspaper and a 14-day notification period and all the rest." [11] The extent of federal mandates has become staggering. Between 1941 and 1970 there were only 178 mandates imposed on local governments, as either conditions for receiving aid or as direct orders—all but 14 of them issued from 1960 to 1970. Between 1971 and 1978, there were 1,079 such federal mandates. [12]

Interpretation of federal regulations varies from jurisdiction to jurisdiction. In addition, agencies often receive funds from several grants for the same general program area, thus complicating compliance reviews. At least in part as a result of these conditions, compliance with federal regulations often is not total. To deny an urban jurisdiction funding for a major program for noncompliance is politically difficult and thus rare.

TENSIONS AMONG GENERAL PURPOSE GOVERNMENTS

A variety of intergovernmental actors is involved in the lobbying efforts on behalf of urban areas. These urban advocates are both public and private sector actors. In particular, they are representatives of public interest groups, members of Congress, state and local officials, and representatives of special districts. Because lobbyists focus not only on the nature of grants, but also on the formulas for distribution of the funds for the program, it might be useful to look at each of these actors separately in order to understand their particular role in the political process as it affects intergovernmental grants to urban areas.

The public sector lobbyists can be divided into several groups and there is not always agreement among them. Public sector urban lobbyists include elected public officials such as governors, mayors, county executives, state administrators, and program directors. Program directors may work for general purpose governments—those providing several services—or for special service districts—as is often the case among education officials. In addition to individual lobbying by these individuals, public interest groups representing their interests also operate to influence the decisionmaking process. Not all mayors, governors, or other urban officials agree; varying conditions in different urban areas have led to policy and program splits among these officials. Some specific examples of this phenomenon will give us a better understanding of exactly how diverse otherwise seemingly similar jurisdictions may respond to the intergovernmental grants process.

Cities *vs.* Counties

The case of cities versus counties is a particularly interesting one. Prior to the passage of general revenue sharing and major block grant programs, counties were not central actors in the provision of federally funded urban services in most sections of the United States. Though there are states where county government was relatively strong, most state laws governing county powers usually provided that counties maintain criminal justice systems, roads, and not much else. Cities, towns, and special districts provided for most other service delivery. Thus most counties—urban and rural—were not very active in trying to influence national policymakers. With the advent of revenue sharing and block grants, counties became direct recipients of federal funds. As such they were granted a new role in urban service delivery and became more central participants in federally funded urban programs.

Though the National Association of Counties (NACO) maintained organizational headquarters in Washington prior to the advent of the block grant and general revenue sharing programs, these programs seem to have activated NACO into the role of a strong lobbying organization. Once county leaders began to see the potential for their expanded role in service delivery, conflict arose between cities and counties as to which jurisdiction was the appropriate provider of services. As population and industry moved out of older central cities and older established suburbs into the areas surrounding these jurisdictions, small towns and villages frequently experienced expansion in their population size and tax base. Frequently, no general purpose government below the county level was in place, and the county was required to deliver primary services. Given this population shift and the new fiscal role for counties provided by general revenue sharing and block grants, it is not surprising that a rift between cities and urban counties began to evolve.

During congressional debate on the Housing and Urban Development Act of 1972, for example, the question arose as to whether or not direct entitlement should be extended to urban counties. The final version of the bill included urban counties as direct entitlement jurisdictions. This inclusion was not, however, accepted without both substantial lobbying efforts by NACO and considerable counter-lobbying activities by cities and other urban communities. The small communities and large cities opposed inclusion of urban counties within the entitlement category because they feared this would reduce the funds directly available for cities and small towns.[13]

Funding for the CETA program provides another example of conflict between city and county. The funding formula for CETA requires that general purpose jurisdictions must have populations of at least 100,000 people to be primary sponsors for programs. Special exceptions may be made by the secretary of the Department of Labor. Wilmington, Delaware, a city with fewer than 80,000 people, is the largest city in the state. The city received an exception to the CETA prime sponsor rule and is a prime sponsor, as is the county in which it is located.

There are 10 states in which the largest cities have populations of fewer than 100,000, but not all of these cities have shared Wilmington's experience in receiving an exception to the prime sponsor rule. Portland, Maine, with a population of less than 100,000, is one of the largest cities in that state. Counties in Maine have very limited powers—their budgets must be approved by the state legislature and they have no direct taxing authority. However, following CETA's designations, the counties in Maine are the prime sponsors for CETA grants.

The county in which Portland is located had a fiscal 1978 budget of $1.9 million to operate the county courts and a rural sheriff's department. It received $9 million in CETA funding. The city of Portland and the neighboring communities had combined budgets of more than $100 million and were responsible for welfare, education, economic development, community development, and a plethora of other urban services and yet it received no direct CETA funds.[14]

Portland's mayor, Bruce A. Taliento, testified before the Senate intergovernmental relations subcommittee that "CETA, in the greater Portland area, is in shambles—it stands isolated and totally un-accountable.... Under CETA, the federal government has created an intergovernmental nightmare in the Greater Portland area, and the only response we'll get from the federal government is one of total indifference."[15] Quite clearly, the prime sponsor rule, which came about as a result of successful county lobbying efforts, can hurt cities such as Portland.

Large Cities *vs.* Small Cities

Splits also occur between large cites and small cities because of their different interests. This division does not receive a great deal of public attention. The resources available for solutions to their problems often are quite different. For example, a large city can afford to maintain skilled staffs or consultants—often with offices in Washington—to keep track of available federal grants and to choose the mechanisms most suitable for the jurisdiction. Futhermore, when competitive grants are available, these jurisdictions submit well-developed applications prepared by trained staff members. Small cities often cannot maintain such staffs. In addition, when grants have formulas which set size specifications for eligibility—as is the case with the CETA or CDBG programs—smaller cities are often prevented from direct participation in programs because of the domination of larger cities. As a result, the smaller cities often support different types of federal grants than do the larger cities. In particular, they generally prefer formula grants that provide direct entitlements or that set aside a specified amount of money for competition among small cities.

Another condition that favors larger cities is that often a member of Congress who comes from that city assumes the responsibility of pursuing city interests. This may mean serving on urban committees or on appropriations subcommittees that fund federal agencies dealing directly with cities. This type of legislator can become an advocate for the city and its funding requests. On the other hand, representatives from predominantly rural districts have not tended to serve on the committees that write a great deal of the grant legislation.

Special Districts

Another set of policy actors who try to influence the intergovernmental grants process are representatives of special districts. Special districts are established to serve a single purpose such as providing for education, sanitation services, water, or transportation. The popularity of special districts as providers of services to urban areas varies from state to state. Special districts often are established in order to provide a flexible unit for service delivery. Thus, special districts may be single county, multi-county, or may not follow county boundaries at all. Special service districts prefer to receive federal funds directly so that administrative and legislative interests in the state, county, or city do not have the discretion to decide how their federal grant dollars should be spent. They prefer that decisions be made by policy specialists in the program area and not by general purpose governments or elected officials. Consequently, their representatives are more likely to lobby for categorical grants than for revenue sharing or block grants, and so may come into direct conflict with cities and counties.

CONCLUSIONS

Urban jurisdictions—North and South, city and county—are very much dependent upon federal aid to ensure their economic viability. In part this dependence is based upon habit. However, habit is not the only reason. The decade of the 1970s witnessed significant shifts in population and industry, as well as the deleterious effects of deferred capital maintenance, which have taken their toll on the fiscal, economic, and social health of urban America.

Between 1970 and 1978 approximately 3 million people moved into rural areas. Also during the 1970s, 2,400 rural counties gained population, and about 350 of these counties grew by more than 16.7 percent between 1970 and 1976—triple the national growth rate. As people moved from large cities into small towns they have demanded the same type of public services they were previously accustomed to—public roads, local schools, hospitals, clinics, and other services. Rural residents traditionally have been philosophically opposed to seeking help from the federal government, but the new rural residents do not adhere to such a philosophy. In fact, small cities and towns have formed their own lobbying organizations in an effort to share in the federal aid pie. As the population has shifted to suburban and rural areas, the decaying urban tax base has contributed to the decline of city facilities and services. Urban areas have looked to federal grants for help; rural areas have also begun to compete for these federal grants.

Conflict has arisen regarding the flow of federal dollars. General revenue sharing and the block grant programs have directed billions of dollars to the subnational governments, and jurisdictions that had not received much federal aid prior to the 1970s became grant recipients. They discovered ways to use these new-found revenues and now perceive continued need for these revenues to fund programs and avoid additional tax increases. It is unlikely that either the demand for federal aid dollars by older jurisdictions or by newly-expanding communities will decline. It also appears that the program fragmentation that has in part been fostered by bargaining, negotiation, and compromise will continue in the foreseeable future.

Direct federal aid to counties will probably continue to grow as more and more counties undergo governmental modernization and expand their services. As the older suburbs and cities continue to lose population, and ultimately congressional representation and clout, their ability to compete for federal grants dollars will decline. The cities may in fact find themselves in the position of aligning themselves with the states; state governments have been relatively generous to their urban jurisdictions when they have been given the responsibility to channel federal aid to localities. It is also likely that the established bureaucratic links between federal agencies and program specialists— the regulators and the regulated—will remain and that the major categorical grants will not be folded into block grants or revenue sharing to general purpose governments. Finally, because of the other competing demands on these dollars, federal money to meet urban needs will become more difficult to obtain, and the conflicts between jurisdictions will increase.

NOTES

1. *Washington Post,* December 27, 1979.
2. The following discussion relies heavily on data reported by Marian Lief Palley and Howard A. Palley, *Urban America and Public Policies,* 2d ed. (Lexington, Mass.: D. C. Heath & Co., 1981), pp. 57-85.

3. Ibid., p. 59.
4. U.S. Advisory Commission on Intergovernmental Relations, *Significant Features of Fiscal Federalism, 1978-79 Edition* (Washington, D.C.: U.S. Government Printing Office, 1979), p. 82.
5. Rochelle Stanfield, "Government Seeks to Write Formula for Community Development Funds," *National Journal,* 9 (February 12, 1977): 240.
6. Rochelle L. Stanfield, "Federal Aid for Cities—Is It a Mixed Blessing?" *National Journal* 10 (June 3, 1978): 870.
7. U.S. Advisory Commission on Intergovernmental Relations, staff computations based on U.S. Bureau of the Census, *City Government Finances in 1957, 1967, and 1978,* (Washington, D.C.: U.S. Government Printing Office), various tables.
8. ACIR, *Significant Features of Fiscal Federalism,* p. 79.
9. U.S., House of Representatives, Committee on Banking, Finance and Urban Affairs, Subcommittee on the City, *Report: City Need and Responsiveness of Federal Grants Programs* (Washington, D.C.: U.S. Government Printing Office, 1978), p. xiii.
10. Richard P. Nathan and Charles F. Adams, *Revenue Sharing: The Second Round* (Washington, D.C.: Brookings Institution, 1979), p. 8.
11. Rochelle L. Stanfield, "Federal Aid—Taking the Good with the Bad," *National Journal* 10 (July 8, 1978): 1080.
12. Rochelle L. Stanfield, "If You Want the Federal Dollars, You Have to Accept the Federal Controls," *National Journal* 12 (January 19, 1980): 106.
13. U.S. Advisory Commission on Intergovernmental Relations, *Community Development: The Workings of a Federal-Local Block Grant* (Washington D.C.: U.S. Government Printing Office, 1977), pp. 22-27.
14. U.S., Senate, Committee on Governmental Affairs, Subcommittee on Intergovernmental Relations, 95th Cong., 2nd sess., pp. 254-262.
15. Ibid., pp. 260-261.

8

Small Towns and
Rural Communities

Small cities, towns, and rural communities have different problems from those of metropolitan areas, even though the distinction between urban and rural areas can be vague. The typical small town does not exist. Small towns are as different from each other as they are from the large cities. Despite the fact that some federal agencies, such as the Farmers Home Administration (FmHA), have developed programs aimed at meeting the needs of small cities, towns, and rural counties, Washington deals with nonmetropolitan areas primarily through programs designed for metropolitan areas. As a result, officials from small communities must deal with complex programs often designed for governments with greater administrative capacity. Often federal officials fail to recognize the diverse needs of small cities and towns; in other cases the communities resist federal assistance. According to the House Subcommittee on the City, "smaller cities face the same problems of their larger counterparts and not infrequently lack the technical skills and institutions to deal with them." [1]

It is important to examine intergovernmental relations in nonmetropolitan areas for several reasons. First, local governments in nonmetropolitan areas far outnumber those in urban areas; 70 percent of all local governments are in rural America. Second, these jurisdictions provide services to approximately 30 percent of America's citizens. More importantly, there is an interdependence of urban and rural problems. From the 1930s to the 1960s, for example, urban areas experienced a heavy in-migration of poor, unskilled workers displaced by the increasing mechanization of agriculture. This increased mechanization and migration accelerated the decline of many small communities in nonmetropolitan areas.

As noted in the previous chapter, there was a reversal of trends in population movement and industrial location during the late 1970s. According to demographer Calvin Beale of the Department of Agriculture, in recent years "nonmetropolitan areas gained 4.2 percent in population compared to only 2.9 percent for metro areas." Decentralization of industry, increased relocation of retired people, greater recreational opportunities, and higher birth rates also played a role in the recent growth of some rural areas.[2] Thus, there is a rapidly growing need for services in a significant number of small communities, many of which are ill-equipped to deal with this sudden expansion.

The definition of *rural* varies among federal agencies. Establishing a fixed upper population limit of 10,000, 20,000, or 50,000, as do many federal programs, is an inadequate measure for several reasons. First, these upper population limits vary widely across programs. Second, some small jurisdictions are located adjacent to large cities, and have many urban features. Finally, small cities in metropolitan areas experience different problems and possess different resources from those located in rural areas. This chapter focuses on small cities that are located outside of the Standard Metropolitan Statistical Areas, and that are fairly independent of large central cities. These communities are defined as nonmetropolitan by the Census Bureau. The terms *rural* and *nonmetropolitan,* as well as the terms *small cities* and *towns,* are used interchangeably throughout this chapter..

Examining intergovernmental relations in small towns and rural communities helps to place the regulatory model of intergovernmental policy in bold relief. Both state and urban governments and officials have a part in constructing the maze of contemporary intergovernmental grants. Small towns and rural governments and their officials are newcomers to this process and are yet too new to be able to be full participants in this system. Put in somewhat different terms, the larger urban jurisdictions often operate from positions of power in the federal system. Their large staffs and political clout translate into concrete advantages during the grant application and program implementation phases of program operations. Small towns and cities operate at a disadvantage in terms of initial awareness, grantsmanship skills, and program implementation. Looking at towns and small cities also forces us to recognize the unique problems of rural America, problems that are not always addressed by existing grant programs.

More specifically, we will look first at the special problems facing nonmetropolitan areas. Then the relationships between smaller jurisdictions and the federal grants process will be discussed. Finally, the attempts to facilitate the delivery of federal aid to rural America will be examined.

THE SPECIAL PROBLEMS OF NONMETROPOLITAN AREAS

Although many Americans hold to idealistic, pastoral views of the rural Americans that are captured in Norman Rockwell's illustrations, severe social problems exist outside metropolitan areas. All too often rural governments lack the tax base or institutional capacity to attack the problems of inadequate water supply, income, or housing; intergovernmental programs can play important roles in rural areas. About 10.5 million persons, 41 percent of the nation's poor, live in rural areas. As shown in Figure 8-1, these people generally are

Fig. 8-1.
Comparative Profile of Poor Households in Metro and Nonmetro Areas, 1975.

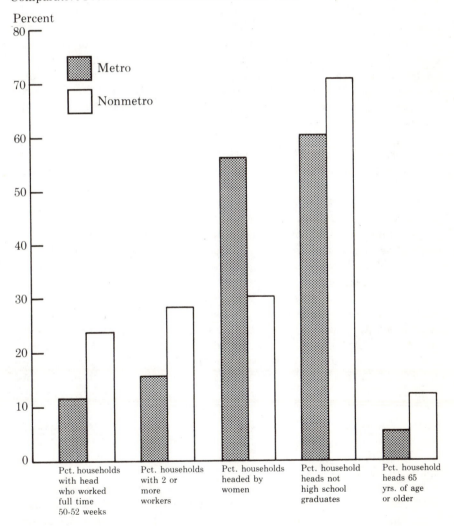

SOURCE: U.S. Bureau of Census.

older, more disabled, and less educated than the urban poor. The lack of adequate housing is a serious problem for many in rural areas, particularly for the elderly. At least 60 percent of the older persons living in rural communities occupy homes dating from the pre-World War I era. Moreover, billions of dollars are needed to upgrade rural water and sewer systems—2 million rural Americans do not have running water, and 13.7 million lack drinking water that meets national safe drinking water standards. Another 2.4 million rural Americans have inadequate sewage disposal facilities, or none at all.

There are also serious problems in the areas of transportation and health care. Although rural residents lose more work days due to chronic illness than do urban residents, they receive a lower share of the nation's health resources. Rural areas have, on a per capita basis, 29 percent fewer nurses, 38 percent fewer dentists, and 58 percent fewer doctors than the nation as a whole. Transportation is a serious problem in nonmetropolitan areas because fewer than 1 percent of rural residents are able to use public transportation to reach their jobs. This forces a dependence on the automobile as a primary mode of transportation. Yet many rural residents— 57 percent of the rural poor—do not own a car. Many others must drive long distances, and pay high gasoline bills, to reach their jobs or basic social services.[3]

In addition to these conditions, it is important to note the diversity of problems faced by small communities. Many small towns are experiencing population and economic decline; from 1970 to 1975, approximately 43 percent of the cities with populations of 25,000 to 50,000 lost residents.[4] However, other small towns, which are often far removed from central cities, are experiencing a "rural renaissance." Improvements in transportation, high urban labor costs, and aging capital plants in urban areas, coupled with rural receptivity to growth, often open up new areas to rapid economic expansion. Yet both the declining small city and the "boom town" often share one thing in common—the inability to manage, or the legal and institutional capacity to cope with, either steady decline or growth. "In rural areas, the issue is the absence of investment. Things like sewers weren't built in the first place," commented a FmHA consultant. Yet many of these same small communities are now being asked to adjust to an unprecedented growth in population by building new roads, bridges, sewers, and social service centers.[5]

Indeed, many local governments are not capable of coping with economic or social problems. One indicator of their lack of capacity is the fact that 89 percent of the local governments have fewer than 50 employees, and 48 percent of these have five or fewer employees.

Fig. 8-2. Number of Fulltime Employees in Special Districts and Municipal and Town Governments.

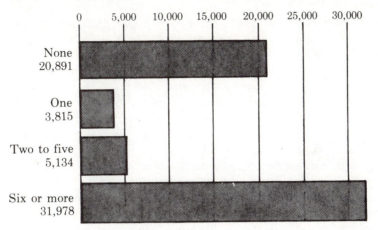

SOURCE: U.S. Bureau of Census.

According to Census Bureau calculations, nearly three-fourths of the towns with populations of fewer than 2,500 run their government on a parttime basis. This fact is clearly ilustrated in Table 8-2. The Advisory Commission on Intergovernmental Relations analyzed the role of local governments in nonmetropolitan areas and found that they need a great deal of help. They are not only limited in the services they can provide, but their unit costs for services are also higher. Additionally, these towns often lack the grantsmanship to compete with larger cities for federal and state aid. Even when assistance is available, limited resources can make it hard to raise matching funds or to repay loans. When growth does occur, local governments cannot always respond in a timely manner. A sudden influx of population may place heavy burdens on an aging infrastructure and create new social and environmental problems.[6]

FEDERAL AID AND NONMETROPOLITAN AREAS

Because of the stresses on towns and small cities, dependence on federal aid jumped drastically during the 1970s. In a study of cities with populations between 25,000 and 50,000, Herrington J. Bryce of the Academy for Contemporary Problems found that the unadjusted flow of funds from the federal government to small cities increased by 800 percent from 1970 to 1978. In 1970 cities with populations between 25,000 and 50,000 received 2.9 percent of their revenue from federal sources; in 1976 federal aid accounted for 12 percent of small city receipts.[7] According to John Ross and John Shannon of the ACIR, growing dependency was "not an exclusive sin of large cities, rather ... the growth of dependency between 1962-1975 of federal aid to small cities ... was almost as large as among cities over one million and more than all other city size classes."[8]

Despite the growth in aid allocations to small cities and rural areas, most small communities still receive less than a proportionate share of federal grants-in-aid. Although federal spending in urban and rural areas is approximately equal on a per capita basis, much of what is spent in rural areas is spent to build highways and subsidize large farmers and not to assist local governments.[9]

Small towns and rural communities have special problems in obtaining federal assistance. In 1975, for example, general revenue sharing funds, which are allocated by formula, accounted for 38 percent of federal aid to all cities—ranging from 53 percent for cities with populations of fewer than 50,000 to 21 percent in cities with populations between 50,000 and 1 million.[10] This disparity underlines the fact that larger communities are securing a greater share of their grant money through categorical and block grant programs. Indeed, size appears to be directly related to grants success. Of the first $2.5 billion in HUD Community Development Block Grant money that went to small cities during the first four years of the program, only 22 percent went to localities with populations of fewer than 5,000 people, even though such places account for 40 percent of the small city poverty population.[11]

Why is it that smaller cities seem to have less success in obtaining federal grants? There are several explanations. Since rural programs often are administered from an urban setting, the isolation of local governments makes them less accessible to federal officials. In fact, because of travel and budget constraints, federal officials tend to focus technical assistance efforts on behalf of large cities.

Lack of information also limits rural participation in the grants process. Until very recently, rural officials were not well-organized. It was not until the 1970s that groups such as the National Association of Towns and Townships, the National Association of Smaller Communities, and the American Association of Small Cities began to operate in Washington. In addition, the National League of Cities and the National Association of Counties recently started to work more closely with smaller communities. Moreover, the complexities of federal regulations require sophisticated staffs that many small towns have been unwilling or unable to hire. These towns may shy away from federal assistance because they lack the capacity to implement federal programs. The paperwork and regulatory burden that follow once grants are received act as a deterrent. In addition, the inability to raise matching funds on grants or to repay loans discourages full participation by many towns and small cities. Finally, some small towns are very conservative fiscally and their citizens feel that it is inappropriate to use federal funds for local programs.

Participation in the Grants System

Although many small cities apply for and receive federal funds, their participation rates are affected by size and staffing. According to a 1979 analysis by B. J. Reed and Roy Green of a National League of Cities (NLC) survey of 989 cities with population levels below 50,000, 84 percent had applied for at least one federal grant in the previous three years, 46 percent had applied for three or more programs, and 18 percent sought five or more grants. However, application rates do vary with size. Those small cities with populations of more than 25,000 apply for and receive aid twice as often as towns with populations under 2,500. On balance, the NLC survey clearly indicates substantial small city participation in federal programs. Local officials most frequently applied for HUD Community Development Block Grants, CETA funds, EDA loans and grants, EPA wastewater treatment grants, and FmHA loans and grants.[12]

In addition to variations in frequency of application and success rates, the programs for which applications for federal assistance are filed vary. For example, Reed and Green found only a moderate relationship between city needs and whether or not they applied for assistance in that program area. They note that, "while local need was an important consideration, equally important or more important were the availability of funding and whether the city knows about the program or has the capacity to apply for it." For example, only 57 percent of the small cities with poor sewer facilities applied for EPA wastewater treatment grants. While need is an important factor, more important determinants are the availability of funding, knowledge about the program, and capacity to submit an application.[13]

The demand for funds is dependent on the knowledge that programs exist. In states that use their entire allotment of FmHA programs, state agencies and private groups often take the lead in promoting the programs. Often FmHA takes the lead in bringing grant programs to small communities that may be unfamiliar with program requirements. Yet in other states understaffing handicaps FmHA in allocating all of its funds. In Pennsylvania FmHA has only marginal success in allocating funds. Perhaps this is the case because there is only one FmHA employee for every 28,000 rural persons, while the national average staff ratio is 1 to 8,500 rural residents.[14]

Lobbying

In response to their fiscal problems, new small city and town lobbies now are operating in Washington. Many rural administrators are learning the federal aid game. Older groups such as the National League of Cities and the National Association of Counties, traditionally dominated by their larger members, have improved efforts to look after their smaller members. As previously noted, since 1976 three groups—the National Association of Towns and Townships, the National Association of Smaller Communities, and the American Association of Small Cities—have opened Washington offices. In fact, many small communities turned to Washington after revenue sharing checks began going to general purpose subnational units of governments. Enticed by this aid, but frustrated by the accompanying red tape, small cities began to search for other types of aid available from the federal government.

These small city groups are trying to increase their knowledge about grants in small cities and towns and to remove barriers to eligibility. Newsletters, seminars, and training are being instituted to keep small city and town officials informed of changes that will affect their funding chances. Another approach is to lobby for changes that will make federal programs more responsive. One goal of the small communities is to increase their direct eligibility for participation in programs distributed by formula. This would help put small cities and towns on a more competitive basis with the large cities, states, and urban counties. Other targets of small city lobbies are red tape and procedural requirements—such as multiple copies of an application—that are expensive for small jurisdictions. Additionally, local officials regularly complain that many federal regulations, clean air or water standards for example, are oriented toward solving problems in urbanized areas. They argue that a small community may be able to combat water pollution with a natural process, such as a lagoon, instead of an expensive wastewater treatment plant. Similarly, they complain that publications such as the *Federal Register* are written in technical jargon that parttime officials may not understand.[15]

Grantsmanship Capacity

Even if the small city lobby successfully removed informational and bureaucratic barriers to full participation in the grants system, another remaining condition still would limit their success. That factor is grantsmanship skill, or the ability to prepare competitive applications. Many rural counties or small cities simply don't have the engineers, accountants, planners, and other resources that are available to larger cities and state governments. The capacity for grantsmanship or grants management is directly related to the ability to identify, secure, and implement federal programs. According to Bryce, without a professional staff, "small cities are at a disadvantage in applying for federal funds; it also means that many of them are dependent on other jurisdictions to do their planning." [16] Because the larger small cities generally are better staffed than the smallest towns, they tend to succeed more in competition for programs like HUD's small cities CDBG awards.

The ACIR found that less than 27 percent of cities with populations between 10,000 and 25,000 had grant-in-aid coordinators, while over 50 percent of the cities with populations of more than 50,000 assigned a fulltime employee to the job.[17] According to the mayor of Carrboro, North Carolina, "Those cities which are fortunate enough to have staff members with grant-writing skills can accumulate a disproportionate share of the available federal monies, while those cities with high levels of need may go unfunded due to their lack of staff expertise." [18] In some towns local officials mix and match grants into sophisticated local development operations, yet towns such as Kings Mountain, North Carolina, and Blades, Delaware, which we discussed in Chapter 5, are still exceptions to the rule. As long as some small towns invest more in staffing than do others, wide variations in success rates will continue. Yet many towns lack the resources to hire even a single consultant. In these cases it may be reasonable to expect the counties, regional groups, or states to provide technical assistance to the community.

Program Duplication

In fact, only a sophisticated manager or consultant can understand the overlap, duplication, and gaps among related federal programs. In the area of water and sewers alone, programs are funded by EPA, EDA, HUD, and FmHA. Local officials must cope with important differences in goals and procedures among these programs. For example, while the other programs all can aid development and economic growth, EPA's construction grant program is aimed at cleaning up existing pollution, not at promoting economic growth. EPA relies on the states to select and monitor projects, while the other agencies work directly with local communities. HUD and EPA rely exclusively on grants; EDA and FmHA, on the other hand, can make loans. Furthermore, the matching rates differ among the programs: EPA— 75 percent; EDA—50 to 80 percent; FmHA—up to 75 percent; HUD— up to 100 percent. Because of limited tax bases, local governments often find it necessary to involve more than one agency to finance a complete project. For instance, Farmers Home Administration loans and grants frequently are used to help reduce the 25 percent local share on EPA wastewater treatment grants. However, once several agencies jointly fund a project, the paperwork burden increases considerably. The White House estimates that millions of dollars could be saved each year if EPA, EDA, FmHA, and HUD imposed only one set of compliance requirements acceptable to all four agencies.[19]

Duplication and overlap among programs overwhelm some parttime officials. According to John W. Robinson, executive director of the Maryland Municipal League, local officials "are in a very real sense voluntary workers for their communities. Some of them are elected; most of them serve because they want to. Certainly, they aren't in it for the money—they probably wouldn't make the minimum wage." [20] Many small communities simply don't have the time or the expertise to develop a project, discuss it with the federal bureaucrats, and produce federal applications and the other paperwork that accompanies every grant. Some smaller towns have trouble attracting federal money because the social and economic data they must use comes from census data that reflects conditions in much larger areas. Small towns need to know how to disaggregate census data if they are to score well during a competitive review of their application.

It is important to note that not all small city officials feel the intergovernmental system overwhelms them. Many of the largest small cities, those with populations greater than 25,000, and some smaller towns, are able to use the federal aid system to their advantage. Once a town has successfully applied for a grant, it may develop the momentum to try again. Once they have successfully managed a grant, that success works in their favor, for federal agencies like to fund towns with a record of success. It seems that the rich get richer, while many of the poor stay poor. Many small communities simply refuse to participate in the federal grants system. When cities know how to make programs work, the overlap and duplication among programs provide a wide range of choices.

The existence of several programs in a functional area like water and sewer development means that there are multiple points of entry into the federal aid system. According to the mayor of Chapel Hill, North Carolina, duplication is "from the local standpoint only, beneficial to the smart shopper." If one agency is not responsive perhaps another will be. Moreover, a locality that can mix and match grants may develop facilities or programs beyond the scope of any one federal agency or program to fund. Revenue sharing and community development block grants can be used as local matching funds for other grants, providing a special incentive to the creative grants manager. For instance, the mayor of the small town of Pittsburgh, California, has noted that, "the existence of a variety of programs for the same type of activity is an advantage in that very expensive programs can be more easily undertaken by having other sources to meet matching requirements, especially where the local availability of funds is limited." [21] For instance, FmHA loans and grants frequently become part of the local match on the larger expensive wastewater treatment projects financed with 75 percent EPA monies. This brings us to another important point. Many small towns lack the capacity to manage several federal grants, once they have received them. This is why many cities receiving aid are more concerned about program regulations than about overlapping programs.

Problems with Program Requirements

Another problem often faced by small cities is that the program requirements that are attached to some grant programs are impossible to achieve. In Appalachia many towns are eliminated from federal housing programs because of prohibitions on building new federally funded homes on sites with a steep grade. But in parts of mountainous Kentucky and West Virginia much of the land is on the sides of mountains.

Rules designed for implementation in metropolitan areas or for national uniformity can raise costs beyond the financial capability of small towns. For example, small town administrators argue that they need relief from the prevailing wage rules of the Davis-Bacon Act. According to Fred Zook, mayor of Ottawa, Kansas, "programs which are designed to reduce unemployment in the city such as local public works become ineffective because most local contractors are excluded from bidding on the project since they cannot afford to pay the wages. Thus, the large city general contractors who are paying the prevailing wages get the jobs." [22]

Even when assistance is available a small town may have trouble raising matching funds, repaying bonds, and operating and maintaining costly municipal facilities such as wastewater treatment plants. In the case of water pollution abatement, conventional methods—collector systems and centralized treatment plants—are not as cost-effective in rural areas as in urban areas. Although a mile of sewer line costs relatively the same regardless of city size, more miles usually will be needed per capita in small cities.

Small towns also have special problems in borrowing funds to finance the local share of EPA projects. The financing problems arise for small communities because they lack ready access to the municipal bond market. The fixed cost of maintenance may also be a larger portion of the municipal budget, and thus often tax increases will be required.

Less costly alternatives to full-scale sewer development do exist; small package treatment plants, land overflow systems, treatment ponds, and marsh-pond systems may be appropriate in some cases. In the 1977 amendments to the Federal Water Pollution Control Act, Congress noted this and did increase incentives for alternative technologies by raising the federal matching share for these projects to 85 percent. Yet to date, EPA has not aggressively promoted lower cost alternatives in rural areas. Even in the planning stage few projects have been reworked to take advantage of appropriate or innovative technologies. Other changes could reduce the costs to small towns. EPA and state environmental agencies are now taking steps to streamline the approval process. This could speed up construction by six months and hold down the effect of inflation on project costs. As things stand now, many EPA wastewater treatment projects impose severe burdens on small towns that have few choices but to comply with national requirements.

Once federal aid is received, the smallest and least experienced cities continue to have trouble. For example, Nathan and Dommel found that prior grant experience was an important factor in conflict resolution between HUD block grant administrators and the cities. They wrote that "Communities with moderate and high levels of previous HUD grant experience were successful about half the time on substantive issues, while those with little or no experience prevailed only 20 percent of the time." [23] This indicates that smaller communities lack the resources of larger cities in the bargaining that goes on as a part of the regulatory process.

In summary, small local governments have severe problems in coping with the system of federal assistance. They find the grants system to be less accessible to them than it is for urban areas. They often lack the resources to compete for the grants for which they are eligible. Further, limited staff and tax bases seriously restrict the number of grant programs they can undertake. Although well-staffed towns can become very adept at mixing and matching federal grants, most small communities are simply overwhelmed and may be unaware of grant money for which they may be eligible. As a result, small towns increasingly are dependent on other groups to do their planning.

EFFORTS TO IMPROVE THE DELIVERY
OF FEDERAL ASSISTANCE

Many local governments now are turning to regional groups or state agencies for assistance and ways to improve the delivery of services to nonmetropolitan America. Some advocate greater coordination or technical assistance roles for substate regional agencies. Others argue that federal rural aid should go through the states. Still others suggest improvements in federal administration as a way to enhance program delivery to small cities and rural counties.

Substate Regionalism

Substate regional bodies often are viewed as an answer to problems of intergovernmental coordination in rural areas. Nonmetropolitan planning development commissions are one way to augment the staffs of small towns that individually cannot afford to hire the necessary staff. Already many towns rely on regional planning groups to prepare applications or coordinate service delivery. In urban areas, regional groups such as Councils of Governments concentrate on coordinating diverse and overlapping services. In rural areas, multi-county planning bodies play a very different role. According to an ACIR report, "Nonmetropolitan regional councils, in contrast to their urban counterparts, are more entrepreneurial, more directly linked with the broader spectrum of community decisionmaking and the everyday politics and operations of their member local governments."[24]

Federal agencies frequently support areawide programs. In 1977, 26 aid programs for areawide planning were available to metropolitan and nonmetropolitan areas. Another four areawide grants dealing with community fire protection, transit assistance, development planning, and resource conservation and development are available to areawide agencies in rural areas only. The problem in nonurban areas as in urban areas is that no government-wide federal policy exists to support comprehensive areawide planning. As a result, not all areawide assistance flows to a single comprehensive regional agency. Nevertheless, some nonurban regional councils have achieved considerable success. In Humbolt County, California, the local association of governments established a circuit rider plan, with five small cities sharing a planner and a city manager. The Southern Iowa Council of Governments has established a seven county rural housing authority to administer federal funds. One planning district commission in Virginia operates a regional solid waste collection program that is simply too large for its member governments to administer. Wayne Anderson, executive director of ACIR, says, "many of these activities are accomplished with federal grants, and regional councils frequently act as grantsmen in securing federal funds for their member local governments."[25]

The emphasis is given to direct technical assistance to local governments. Often regional councils in nonmetropolitan areas, unlike metropolitan areas, are the sole source of expertise on how to identify, apply for, and administer grants. The regional planning bodies play an important role in transferring information, developing grantsmanship skills, and actually obtaining grants. Indeed, one study of substate regional bodies in Georgia concludes, "in many areas the regional commissions are the only agencies with the necessary expertise to deal with local problems. It is not uncommon for rural commission staffs to be engaged in all phases of program development." [26] Many nonurban planning groups play a direct entrepreneurial role for their member governments.

As things now stand, the federal government could take several steps to support regional councils. However, today, as Wayne Anderson of the ACIR says, "the federal areawide programs spawn competing, often single-function, regional organizations in almost every substate district of the nation." [27] In fact, many contain from four to six federally sponsored regional bodies. Rather than promoting coordination, federal agencies have contributed to the fragmentation of local government in rural areas. A unified federal aid policy toward regional councils could give them the functional scope needed to coordinate federal aid programs and to assist local governments. Indeed, in 1978 the House Subcommittee on the City, chaired by Democrat Henry S. Reuss of Wisconsin, recommended giving these groups greater support: "the executive branch should rationalize the system of substate agencies encouraged by federal law and regulations." Further, the subcommittee concluded that, "preference should be given to those substate agencies which are politically responsible to the people they serve." [28]

Federal coordination alone cannot give rural regional commissions the lead in coordinating services; they need staffing if they are to perform an outreach function. As things now stand, substate regional planning agencies vary widely in their level of professionalism. Some local officials support the general concept of regional commissions but are reluctant to work directly with regional bodies. This is why many regional bodies emphasize their role in providing technical assistance to local officials. According to a 1978 GAO study, only 21 percent of the cities with populations of fewer than 100,000 and 28 percent of the counties with populations of fewer than 100,000 frequently contact substate regional planning agencies for technical assistance.[29] There clearly is room for improvement.

The Role of the States

The states also have a role to play in aiding small city development and grants management. In the area of technical assistance, for example, state community affairs agencies assist local governments. However, according to a GAO survey, small cities are more likely to turn to substate agencies than to state or federal agencies. Only

15 percent of the cities with populations of fewer than 100,000 regularly turn to state agencies for technical assistance.[30]

State governments also play a role in intergovernmental grants management because in many federal programs they pass through funds to substate governments. According to a 1974 survey of 22 states conducted by the National Association of State Budget Officers and the ACIR, 41 percent of the federal aid coming to those states was channeled to localities. Pass-through funds were heavily concentrated in the areas of public welfare and education—more than 90 percent of the total pass-through funds related to those functions. The remaining 10 percent of the pass-through funds covered a wide variety of functional areas: highways, health, criminal justice, housing, and community development. Thus, since the bulk of the public welfare grants go to the counties, and school districts receive most of the education pass-through funds, comparatively little of the state pass-through funds go directly to the municipalities and townships to administer.[31]

Aside from their pass-through role the states play an important role in the delivery of services. Local governments are a legal creation of the states, and the capacity of localities to govern often is dependent upon state decisions on debt limitations, governmental structure, and annexation powers, as well as state aid programs. Yet a problem exists; officials in many small cities and towns as well as those from large cities do not trust the states. To some local officials, the states represent just another level of red tape. Indeed, one reason why the federal government now provides more direct grants to small communities than in the past is that the states often were perceived by local officials to be unresponsive to rural and urban needs. An ACIR report argues that states have not helped local governments confront the problems they face. "On the whole, state governments are far from doing a fully adequate job of equipping their local governments with adequate fiscal functional, organizational, and areal authority." [32] In fact, lack of response has encouraged lobbyists for small communities to step up their direct appeals for federal aid.

Despite substantial progress in streamlining administrative structures and modernizing state legislatures, comparatively few states are now ready to assist local governments. State efforts to become attentive to local concerns are still in the formative stages, and only in the past several years have the states started to make progress in developing local assistance initiatives, particularly in fields of economic and community development.

There has been considerable regional variation in the emphasis of the new state community assistance efforts. Northeastern and midwestern states have focused on urban development. The southern states, on the other hand, gave priority to developmental needs in declining rural areas and small communities. In the West, the emphasis has been on helping small communities cope with the rapid industrialization associated with new energy development. Nonetheless, serious obstacles, such as state constitutional challenges to new enabling legislation and the expense involved in development efforts, may affect the states' ability to implement local aid programs.[33]

Because of vast differences in the power and capacity of state governments, it is unlikely that the states alone can respond to the needs of small communities. And clearly, any federal effort to channel assistance to localities through the states will result in uneven responses. As a practical matter, each federal agency cannot deal directly with every local government. Federal agencies and Congress could take steps to bring the states aboard as full partners in the implementation of rural programs. This might encourage the states to improve their local relations and increase their fiscal and technical assistance to small communities. Many localities still distrust the states, however, preferring instead to have direct pipelines to federal agencies.

Federal Efforts to Help Rural Areas

In Washington, federal officials are beginning to take notice of the special problems of small cities. Congress has become willing to reserve specific proportions of grant funds for rural areas. HUD's Urban Development Action Grant Program has a 25 percent rural set-aside. In addition to such set-asides, federal policy has begun to take steps toward streamlining grants assistance and enhancing federal coordination in rural areas. Another recent development is a shift in perception about the role of the states. The Congressional Rural Caucus and the ACIR, as well as a few other groups, have argued that the states may be logical intermediaries between the federal establishment and small towns. They maintain that the federal government has not handled its responsibilities toward small cities and town successfully.

As long as only a few small towns were grant recipients, the federal government could manage the situation. But now that revenue sharing and Community Development Block Grants have brought aid to thousands of small cities and towns, which once were independent of direct federal aid, the success of federal rural programs is being questioned. "It is one thing for the federal government to write general revenue sharing checks to thousands of local governments," according to Rochelle Stanfield, "but can it administer the complex array of categorical programs?"[34] Already many federal administrators are severely burdened by agency requirements to visit and provide technical assistance to isolated and widely separated small towns. Not only are local officials bewildered by the array of grant programs, but federal officials are overwhelmed by the large number of jurisdictions with which they must deal. Administrators at EPA, FmHA, and HUD cannot fully understand the serious fiscal, legal, organizational, and political differences that characterize each small town's capacity for grants management.

The National Governors' Association also is asking for a strong state coordinating role. Yet few states—specifically, California, Massachusetts, Michigan, Minnesota, and North Carolina—have played a leadership role in local affairs. President Carter advocated a strong state role, but his urban policy and subsequent rural initiatives largely ignored the states. Congress has remained suspicious of the state role. The local lobbies do not trust the states and "are much stronger than the state lobby and would fight to retain the direct relationship that new constituents already have with the federal government." [35] In short, there may be little effective federal support for a strong state role in coordinating federal aid to local government.

Yet some critics argue that the states could make a positive contribution if only the federal government relied more heavily on them to pass money through to small localities. Because federal formulas, such as that for revenue sharing, do not take into account individual differences among local governments in decisions on the criteria for eligibility for direct aid, money often goes to governments with few fulltime employees. This is shown more clearly in Table 8-2, discussed earlier in this chapter. G. Ross Stephens and Gerald Olson found that 11,000 units of government that lack even one fulltime employee receive revenue sharing allocations. Since the states are better able to determine which counties, municipalities, and townships have responsibilities for public services, and which do not, better targeting of aid to small communities with program responsibilities might result from active state participation in some formula based programs. [36]

Another federal aid reform that might help rural communities would be a shift from categorical to block grants. But since 1974 Congress has not enacted any new block grants, and the number of categorical grants continues to grow. Clearly, the small city lobby wants more flexible aid and less red tape. In 1980 a bill was proposed by Senator John Danforth, Republican from Missouri, to give small cities more flexibility in the use of federal aid. The bill would have allowed cities with populations of fewer than 50,000 to apply for no-strings grants equal to the average amount of federal aid they received during the previous five years. Congress is beginning to understand nonmetropolitan problems, but political support for streamlining rural assistance has not yet produced many results.

Another was to help small cities is to improve program coordination and to simplify the grants process. This would allow small jurisdictions to better compete for, and manage, project grants. The Carter administration's Small Community and Rural Development Policy made a modest start in this direction. One goal outlined by President Carter in his December 1979 policy declaration was to "make federal programs more accessible to rural jurisdictions and community-based organizations, better adapted to rural circumstances and needs, better coordinated, and more streamlined in their administration." Although all jurisdictions want grant simplification, the smallest jurisdictions are the least able to cope with existing red tape.

President Carter's Small Community and Rural Development Policy created a working group, composed of officials at the assistant secretary level, to improve small city access to federal programs. President Carter also asked Congress to create a new position of Under Secretary of Agriculture for Small Community and Rural Development. He invited the nation's governors to establish rural development councils and directed the Federal Regional Councils to cooperate in developing joint federal-state funding strategies. Members of President Carter's cabinet were asked to review departmental programs and improve responsiveness to rural needs.

President Carter's policy statement also listed approximately 150 newly coordinated rural initiatives in the areas of health, housing, water and sewer services, education, social services, and economic development that had been initiated since 1977. One rural initiative, announced in December 1978, involved inter-agency—Environmental Protection Agency, Economic Development Administration, Housing and Urban Development, and Farmers Home Administration—coordination in the delivery of water and sewer programs. This agreement identified many areas where coordination and a single set of requirements—application forms, audits, payment procedure, and environmental compliance rules—could be instituted.[37]

During the Carter administration grant simplification was not forthcoming. There was no major grants simplification legislation nor new rural programs enacted by Congress.

CONCLUSIONS

Small town America increasingly is turning to the federal government for assistance, yet large cities continue to attract most of the attention. Although pressing social problems exist in small towns, they often get lost in the shuffle. Small towns and cities have unique eligibility, application, and implementation problems in the federal grants area. Because they lack the political clout that comes with size, and the sophistication and knowledge that can come with staffing, rural areas must struggle through the federal assistance maze. Many small cities and towns are dependent on technical assistance from other levels of government, and regional, state, and federal agencies have only begun to step up their technical assistance efforts.

Local governments in rural areas need more than technical assistance and major improvements in the attitudes and activities of federal and state agencies. There is a growing awareness at both of these levels of government that small communities are not as independent as they once were. Whether or not either level of government makes an extra effort on behalf of rural jurisdictions depends on the ability of nonmetropolitan governments to become more active participants in the processes of negotiation, bargaining, and compromise, which are central to the contemporary intergovernmental grants process. These governments must recognize the nature of the regulatory-like process that now prevails for intergovernmental grants, and they must be willing and able to become players in this system.

NOTES

1. U.S., House of Representatives, Committee on Banking, Finance and Urban Affairs, Subcommittee on the City, *Report: Small Cities: How Can the Federal and State Governments Respond to Their Diverse Needs?* (Washington, D.C.: U.S. Government Printing Office, 1978), p. 1.
2. Calvin L. Beale, *The Revival of Population Growth in Nonmetropolitan America* (Washington, D.C.: U.S. Department of Agriculture, Economic Research Service, 1976), pp. 3-6.
3. Warren Brown, "Nation's Rural Poor Shortchanged on Public Assistance, Report Says," *Washington Post,* February 28, 1979; U.S., Executive Office of the President, *Rural Development Initiatives: Making Water & Sewer Programs Work* (Washington, D.C.: U.S. Government Printing Office, 1978), p. 1; and U.S., Executive Office of the President, *Small Community and Rural Development Policy* (Washington, D.C.: U.S. Government Printing Office, 1979), p. 3.
4. U.S., House of Representatives, Committee on Banking, Finance and Urban Affairs, Subcommittee on the City, *Hearings: Small Cities, How Can the Federal and State Governments Respond to Their Diverse Needs?* (Washington, D.C.: U.S. Government Printing Office, 1978), p. 43.
5. "Rural America Also Could Use Some Repairs," *Washington Post,* December 28, 1979.
6. House Committee on Banking, *Hearings: Small Cities,* p. 122.
7. Herrington J. Bryce, *Current Trends in Financing Smaller Cities* (Columbus, Ohio: Academy for Contemporary Problems, 1978), p. 16.
8. John Shannon and John Ross, "Cities: Their Increasing Dependence on State and Federal Aid," in *Small Cities in Transition,* ed. Herrington J. Bryce (Cambridge, Mass.: Ballinger Publishing Co., 1977), p. 194.
9. House Committee on Banking, *Report: Small Cities,* pp. 15-18.
10. Shannon and Ross, "Cities," p. 196.

11. For a review of this program, see Rural America, Inc., *CDBG And Small Cities: Funding Patterns, FY 75-78* (Washington, D.C.: Rural America, Inc., 1979).

12. B. J. Reed and Roy E. Green, "City Management and Perceptions of Grants Administration in Smaller Cities" (Paper presented at the Annual Meeting of the Southern Political Science Association, Atlanta, Georgia, November 9-11, 1978), pp. 9-10. See also B. J. Reed and Roy E. Green, "A Perspective on Small City Development: Local Assessments of Grants Management Capacity" (Paper presented at the Annual Meeting of the American Political Science Association, Washington, D.C., Aug. 31-Sept. 3, 1979), pp. 16-18.

13. Ibid., p. 15.

14. Jon Clark and Charles Soria, *The Regional Impact of the Rural Development Act* (Washington, D.C.: Northeast-Midwest Institute, 1979), p. 11.

15. Rochelle L. Stanfield, "Small Cities Are On the Prowl for Help in Washington," *National Journal* 10 (October 7, 1978): 1597-1601.

16. Herrington Bryce, *Planning for Small Cities* (Lexington, Mass.: Lexington Books, 1979), p. 9.

17. U.S. Advisory Commission on Intergovernmental Relations, *The Intergovernmental Grants System as Seen by Local, State and Federal Officials* (Washington, D.C.: U.S. Government Printing Office, 1977), p. 45.

18. Reed and Green, "City Management," p. 13.

19. Executive Office of the President, *Rural Development Initiatives: Making Water and Sewer Programs Work,* pp. 13-15.

20. Tony Upton, "Small City Officials: A New, Welcome Aid Concept," *Government Executive* (April 1979), p. 45.

21. Reed and Green, "City Management," p. 24.

22. House Committee on Banking, *Hearings: Small Cities,* p. 66.

23. Richard P. Nathan and Paul R. Dommel, "Federal-Local Relations Under Block Grants," *Political Science Quarterly* 93 (Fall 1978): 442.

24. U.S. Advisory Commission on Intergovernmental Relations, *Regional Decision Making: Two Strategies for Substate Districts,* Vol. 1 (Washington, D.C.: U.S. Government Printing Office, 1978), p. 270.

25. House Banking Committee, *Hearings: Small Cities,* p. 132.

26. Lewis G. Bender, "Substate Regionalism: The Rural Perspective" (Paper presented at the Annual Meeting of the Southern Political Science Association, Atlanta, Georgia, November 9-11, 1978), p. 7.

27. House Committee on Banking, *Hearings: Small Cities,* p. 135.

28. House Committee on Banking, *Report: Small Cities,* p. 21.

29. U.S., General Accounting Office, *State and Local Government Views on Technical Assistance* (Washington, D.C.: U.S. Government Printing Office, 1978), p. 39.

30. Ibid.

31. U.S. Advisory Commission on Intergovernmental Relations, *The State and Intergovernmental Aids* (Washington, D.C.: U.S. Government Printing Office, 1977), pp. 21-23.

32. U.S. Advisory Commission on Intergovernmental Relations, "Federal and State Roles in Building the Capacity of Subordinate Units," in *The White House Conference on Balanced National Growth and Economic Development,* Vol. 6 (Washington, D.C.: U.S. Government Printing Office, 1978), p. 278.

33. U.S. Advisory Commission on Intergovernmental Relations, *State Community Assistance Initiatives: Innovations of the Late 70's* (Washington, D.C.: U.S. Government Printing Office, 1979), pp. 1-9.
34. Rochelle L. Stanfield, "Toward an Urban Policy with a Small-Town Accent," *Publius* 9 (Winter 1979): 40.
35. Ibid., p. 42.
36. John Herbers, "U.S. Funds Go to Towns Said to Lack Real Needs," *New York Times*, November 18, 1979, p. 1.
37. Executive Office of the President, *Small Community and Rural Development Policy*, p. 18.

9

Federalism and the Grants System

As we have shown, the nature of the intergovernmental grants process changed markedly during the 1960s and the 1970s. Not only did the scope of supported activities expand, but so too did the methods by which funds were provided. The number of recipients of aid also increased, complicating the bargaining, negotiation, and compromise process that surrounds intergovernmental policymaking and administration. These changes will be considered briefly here as we review the politics of the intergovernmental grants process. We also will reassess the relevance of a regulatory model and consider the prospects for the future of federal grants to subnational jurisdictions.

FEDERAL GRANTS AND AMERICAN POLITICS

Most of our major national decisionmaking organizations and institutions—political parties, interest groups, Congress, and the bureaucracy—are characterized by fragmentation. As a result, public policy is made in specialized forums, and not in a comprehensive fashion. The present intergovernmental grants system stands as a product of this haphazard and piecemeal policy process. The rapid expansion and proliferation of federal grant programs during the past two decades reflects the basic nature of American politics. The grants system, in turn, further complicates the tasks of domestic government by reinforcing the fragmentation within American politics.

The creation of major new federal grant programs in the 1960s and 1970s encouraged the creation and expansion of public interest groups in Washington. The rise of intergovernmental lobbyists then created pressures for new and expanded programs. These new intergovernmental lobbyists joined the tidal wave of interest groups threatening to displace national political parties in the agenda-setting and decisionmaking process.

165

The number of grant programs and the complexity of their rules and regulations reinforces the role of administrators at all levels of government. Elected state and local officials increasingly find that program specialists in the departments control the implementation of federal grant programs. At the national level, individual members of Congress have supported the system and benefited from this support. These members, operating within an increasingly decentralized and permissive system, act as entrepreneurs and as salespeople for particular programs. In part because of the role of individual members of Congress in program initiation, Congress as an institution has contributed to the crazy-quilt pattern of the intergovernmental grants system, in which everyone has "a piece of the action," but no one is in charge.

In addition to reinforcing the power of program specialists, the intergovernmental grants system also reflects a changing balance of power among subnational governments. At one time the states were the only major grant recipients in the federal grants system. Today, however, direct aid to localities represents a substantial portion of federal aid. Two developments—the urban crisis and the modernization of many county and rural governments—created pressures for this direct federal aid. Programs were reoriented to provide direct aid not only to large cities, but also to urban counties and rural governments as well. New groups were formed and old ones were reorganized around the goal of attracting federal aid. As a result, many federal grants now bypass the states and go directly to thousands of units of local government.

The intergovernmental grants system grew in response to changing political attitudes and economic needs, and that growth was influenced by a number of factors in American politics. Weak political parties, decentralized policymaking in Congress, strong interest groups, administrative discretion, and weak state governments helped to shape the increasingly fragmented grants system.

REGULATORY POLITICS
AND INTERGOVERNMENTAL GRANTS

We suggested that the intergovernmental grants process was similar in a variety of ways to the business regulatory system. In particular, we have noted three phenomena: 1) groups outside of the national political decisionmaking process often make demands on national decisionmakers; 2) the regulating agencies and regulated organizations become interdependent; and 3) federal influence is limited. These conditions prevail in the government regulation of businesses and appear to have evolved in the federal intergovernmental grants system. There are many reasons for this. For example, the decline of the political party system in the 1970s, and the subsequent decreased value of party loyalty, led to expanded public lobbying. As the congressional seniority system began to crumble and committees spawned subcommittees, new political leadership centers evolved, and more and more access points into the congressional system became available. Additionally, as Congress became more fragmented and more specialized, it became easier for regulated groups—often state or local elected officials or, even more frequently, program specialists—to capture the attention of a particular subcommittee or administrative unit.

In addition to these structural conditions, other situations fostered change. During the years of the Johnson and Nixon administrations, grants programs grew at a very healthy pace. General revenue sharing, CETA, and Community Development Block Grants made many general purpose local jurisdictions directly eligible for federal grants. With these new participants came new competition and a need for enhanced grantsmanship skills. To protect their stake in the intergovernmental system, program specialists and big city mayors—followed by county executives, governors, and rural officials—expanded their role as active lobbyists.

Furthermore, the nation's economic instability during the 1970s took its toll on the states and the localities. From the relative prosperity of the early 1970s, the nation experienced the beginnings of a recession in the middle of the decade. As states and localities began to recoup their losses, antitax and anti-public spending moods swept the country in 1978 and 1979, and a deep recession in 1980 added to their economic woes. When economic conditions are uncertain, subnational jurisdictions attempt to gain a competitive edge in obtaining federal resources.

During the 1970s, large cities, urban counties, and small towns became more dependent on federal aid. Only the state governments failed to show a dramatic increase in federal aid as a percentage of total revenue. This growing fiscal dependence also parallels regulatory politics. Many private firms have become dependent on regulatory agencies to protect them from competition, and the federal grants process works in the same way, in effect, to insulate public programs from having to compete for local or state funding. Thus, in both the public and private arenas we find officials trying to have their cake and eat it too; that is, publicly criticizing federal intrusion while simultaneously resisting proposals to deregulate activities or terminate federal funding.

The groups that maintain lobbying organizations and personnel in Washington, D.C., gain varying degrees of access to congressional and administrative decisionmakers. The public interest groups are

relatively successful in influencing congressional decisionmakers because they represent constituent interests. Administrative influence
is more variable. In fact, representatives of particular general purpose
jurisdictions seem to be less effective at this stage of the policy
process than are the representatives of the specialist groups who
maintain administrator-to-administrator relationships in areas such
as education, public welfare, and housing. An agency such as HUD,
which sees a specific type of elected official—such as mayors of
large cities—as major clients, may be an exception to this rule. However,
most other agencies—such as the departments of Education, Health
and Human Services, and Labor—do not identify with elected officials
as strongly as they do with program specialists. As a result, the
elected officials from general purpose jurisdictions prefer broad-based
grants with formula allocations since they have better access to congressional decisionmakers than to bureaucrats. Yet Congress and federal
administrators resist the deregulation associated with the move from
categorical to broad-based block grants.

It has been suggested that like regulatory politics, intergovernmental programs involve reciprocal influence rather than total control
by the federal government. Intergovernmental grants focus on broad
national goals—effecting changes in the actions of thousands of jurisdictions—and set ambitious goals of developing national programs,
eliminating fiscal disparities, and altering state and local programs.
Oftentimes, the regulations that are part of a grant package attempt
to effect broad scale change in behavior. For example, equal employment guidelines, civil rights regulations, and environmental restrictions are all attempts to bring about policy change. Program-
specific regulations also are aimed at changing state and local policy.
The interplay of grant demands may make compliance difficult for
receiving jurisdictions, and the aid recipients often interpret federal
rules and regulations differently. Also, because of the fungibility involved with many grants, some jurisdictions can maintain federally
funded programs while evading regulatory control. The larger the
jurisdiction, and the greater the number of grants, the more influence
the grantee may have.

Finally, it has been suggested that federal control is limited
in the regulation of both private sector enterprises and subnational
governments. One reason for this is the influence of the public interest
groups and program specialists in the congressional arena. Program
specialists influence congressional committee and subcommittee members in their specific policy area, and these issue-specific client groups
maintain close links to the regulation writers and program specialists
in the federal agencies. The presence of congressional oversight, as
well as the efforts by grantees to influence decisionmakers at all

stages of the implementation process, means that federal agencies frequently must adapt their behavior to local priorities. Because grant recipients are one source of political support for an agency or its programs, state and local governments, and representatives of their program-specific agencies, often co-opt federal officials just as industry is often thought to "capture" its regulators. Grants administration becomes a two-way street where both the regulatory agency and the regulated enterprise exercise imperfect control over the other party.

PROSPECTS FOR THE FUTURE

It is always dangerous to forecast because of the complications of unanticipated developments. Nevertheless, it is necessary to assess the prospects for the future of the relationship between federal and subnational governments in the grants system. General revenue sharing and block grants established a new federal relationship with cities, towns, and counties eligible for direct federal assistance. A new set of *direct* federal-local ties evolved, and the states ceased to be the primary jurisdictional beneficiaries of federal aid. These new actors in the federal grants arena will continue as active participants and direct recipients of federal aid. Their continued role in the federal relationship will be fostered by an expansion of their lobbying activities.

The real dollar value of federal aid peaked in 1978 and declined in 1979 and 1980 in the face of continued inflationary pressures. It seems likely that rising defense spending and entitlement payments to individuals—such as Social Security Insurance—will continue to squeeze the grants sector. Efforts to cut revenue sharing during 1980 signaled the beginning of more difficult times for grant recipients. Grants to state and local governments already have trailed inflation for a few years. Jurisdictions will be competing for fewer real dollars, which will force them to increase their lobbying activities in the intergovernmental grants process. An increase in the number of jurisdictions, such as small towns and rural counties, competing for discretionary grants means that more units will be chasing fewer real dollars. Thus, we can expect stiffer competition between individual jurisdictions, regions, and various public interest groups and programs. The existing coalitions among the public interest groups may fracture as they compete against one another for their share of the federal aid pie, and as the gains to be made become smaller.

While federal grants dollars may not increase in real terms, categorical grants will continue to predominate over broad-based block grants because of the strong influence of specialist interests over agency and congressional decisionmakers. Given the close interaction between congressional subcommittees, agency staffs, and public interest groups, Congress will continue to fund the narrow programs with intense support. As long as Congress remains highly decentralized, broad-based grants, like general revenue sharing and some of the block grants with diffuse benefits, may have a tough time. They are easier targets for would-be budget cutters because they do not elicit intense, focused support among key special interest groups and subcommittee members. For example, Congress has dropped the broad-based antirecession program and has cut funds for one major block grant—the Omnibus Crime and Safe Streets Act. Additionally, support in Congress for revenue sharing has eroded seriously in recent years. Thus, categorical grants are likely to account for as large a portion of intergovernmental transfers in the 1980s as they did in the 1970s.

Even if there is a decrease in the scope or the number of regulations and requirements tied to federal grants, recipient governments will continue to be subject to a variety of programmatic regulations. National policy goals will be partially met by these regulations. The reach of federal policy will continue to exceed its grasp. However, when thousands of governments are subject to regulatory oversight, and there are limited monitoring resources, it is unrealistic to expect that state or local compliance will be uniform. Most agencies simply lack the personnel to insure compliance in every cross-cutting regulatory area; others may lack the inclination.

Originally we suggested that the functions of the three levels of government are no longer clearly separated. Their revenue sources are both interdependent and overlapping, and there often is a wide gulf between the point of decision and the visibility of governmental action. This pattern will continue in the 1980s, and the basic questions posed at the outset of this volume, "Who governs?" and "Does it work?" will be even more difficult to answer. It is important to note that the fragmented nature of American politics and the regulatory process operating within each separate policy area create a very permissive system. While the problems of the present federal grants system are well documented, it is not clear that changing public attitudes, a politically conservative administration, or new fiscal constraints will lead to new patterns of more comprehensive public policymaking and implementation.

Selected Bibliography

The books listed below may be useful to readers who would like to explore further the subjects discussed in this book.

Books

Derthick, Martha. *The Influence of Federal Grants: Public Assistance in Massachusetts.* Cambridge: Harvard University Press, 1970.

Elazar, Daniel J. *American Federalism: A View From the States.* New York: T.Y. Crowell Co., 1972.

Glendening, Parris and Reeves, Mavis Mann. *Pragmatic Federalism.* Pacific Palisades, Calif.: Palisades Publishers, 1977.

Haider, Donald. *When Governments Come to Washington.* New York: Free Press, 1974.

Nathan, Richard R. and Adams, Charles. *Revenue Sharing: The Second Round.* Washington, D.C.: Brookings Institution, 1979.

Wright, Deil. *Understanding Intergovernmental Relations.* North Scituate, Mass.: Duxbury Press, 1978.

Reports

U.S. Advisory Commission on Intergovernmental Relations, *Block Grants: A Comparative Analysis.* Washington, D.C.: U.S. Government Printing Office, 1977.

———. *Categorical Grants: Their Role and Design.* Washington, D.C.: U.S. Government Printing Office, 1977.

———. *Improving Federal Grants Management.* Washington, D.C.: U.S. Government Printing Office, 1977.

———. *The Intergovernmental Grants System As Seen By Local, State, and Federal Officials.* Washington, D.C.: U.S. Government Printing Office, 1977.

U.S., General Accounting Office. *Perspectives on Intergovernmental Policy and Fiscal Relations.* Washington, D.C.: U.S. Government Printing Office, 1979.

U.S., House of Representatives, Committee on Banking, Finance and Urban Affairs, *Hearings: Small Cities: How Can the Federal and State Governments Respond to Their Diverse Needs?* Washington, D.C.: U.S. Government Printing Office, 1978.

U.S., Office of Management and Budget. *Strengthening Public Management in the Intergovernmental System.* Washington, D.C.: Executive Office of the President, 1975.

Articles

Beer, Samuel. "The Adoption of General Revenue Sharing." *Public Policy* 24 (1976): 125-195.

Grodzins, Morton. "The Federal System." *American Government: Readings and Cases.* Edited by Peter Woll. Boston: Little, Brown & Co., 1972.

Hale, George E. and Palley, Marian Lief. "Federal Grants to the States: Who Governs?" *Administration and Society* 11 (1979): 3-26.

Hamilton, Edward K. "On Nonconstitutional Management of a Constitutional Problem." *Daedalus* 107 (1978): 111-128.

Ingram, Helen. "Policy Implementation Through Bargaining: The Case of Federal Grants-in-Aid." *Public Policy* 25 (1977): 501-526.

Monypenny, Phillip. "Federal Grants-in-Aid to State Governments: A Political Analysis." *National Tax Journal* 13 (1960): 1-16.

Walker, David B. "A New Intergovernmental System in 1977." *Publius* 8 (1978): 101-116.

Stanfield, Rochelle L. "Federal Aid For Cities—Is It a Mixed Blessing?" *National Journal* 11 (1978): 868-872.

———. "Small Cities Are on the Prowl For Help from Washington." *National Journal* 10 (1978): 1597-1601.

Index